·TESCO·COOKERY·COLLECTION·

FREEZING

TESCO

Published exclusively for Tesco Stores Ltd,
Delamare Road, Cheshunt, Herts, EN8 9SL
by Cathay Books, 59 Grosvenor Street, London W1

First published 1985

ISBN 0 86178 306 9

Printed in Hong Kong

ACKNOWLEDGEMENTS

The publishers would like to thank the following companies
for their kindness in providing materials and equipment
used in the photography for this book.
David Mellor, 4 Sloane Square, London SW1;
Elizabeth David, 46 Bourne Street, London SW1

We would also like to thank the following who
were concerned in the preparation of the book.

Series Art Director Pedro Prá-Lopez
Editor Jenni Fleetwood
Photographer Laurie Evans with *stylist* Sue Russell
Food prepared for photography by Michelle Thomson

CONTENTS

NOTE

Standard spoon measurements are used in all recipes

1 tablespoon (tbls) = one 15 ml spoon
1 teaspoon (tsp) = one 5 ml spoon
All spoon measures are level

All eggs are sizes 3 or 4 (standard) unless otherwise stated.

For all recipes, quantities are given in both
metric and imperial measures. Follow either set
but not a mixture of both, as they are not interchangeable.

We set up our Consumer Advisory Service in response to the many pleas for information and cooking ideas we received from our customers. It is run by our team of qualified home economists who answer queries, offer practical advice on cookery and the home and give talks and demonstrations on new products and equipment.

The resounding success of the service and the continued demand for more and more recipes and information has now prompted us to produce our own special range of Tesco Cookery Books.

Our series starts with 12 books, each one focusing on an area that our customers have shown particular interest in. Each book contains practical background information on the chosen subject and concentrates on a wide selection of carefully tested recipes, each one illustrated in colour.

Freezing deals with this now well-established kitchen aid in a refreshingly simple way. Introductory tips and tables help you to freeze fresh produce at its best – as and when available – while the recipe section shows you how to cook from your freezer, instead of just using it for leftovers and emergencies. Every recipe contains both a freezing and a serving tip, and there is a menu-selected chapter full of delicious ideas on how best to entertain from your freezer.

I very much hope you will enjoy looking through the pages which follow, trying out the recipes and above all tasting and enjoying the results. Happy Cooking!

Carey Dennis.

Carey Dennis, senior home economist, Tesco Stores Ltd.

INTRODUCTION

An empty freezer can be an exciting challenge or a daunting prospect. This book concentrates on helping it to be the former – with recipes for dishes of all kinds plus basic information to help you use your freezer to the full.

Making the most of your freezer

There are no fixed rules as to what a freezer should or should not contain. What matters is that it should be adapted to its owner's lifestyle.

Freezer space is precious – use it wisely. Before filling your freezer for the first time, or re-stocking it after letting supplies run down, it's a good idea to draw up a list of personal priorities. Do your family eat a lot of meat or enjoy a wide variety of vegetables? Does your job leave little time for preparing family meals or do you entertain a lot?

Do your family love your home baking? If so, it's a good idea to batch-bake loaves of bread and rolls, scones, cakes and pies and store them away in the freezer. Other foods, such as sauces and casseroles, may be successfully batch-cooked, and many people find this an invaluable way of cutting down on day-to-day cooking as well as fuel bills.

Work out how much space you should sensibly devote to convenience foods. For example, more freezer space may be needed for these if you have young children who demand these foods *ad infinitum*. Many convenience foods can be bought in bulk from supermarkets or freezer centres at excellent prices: provided you can spare the freezer space, bulk-buying family favourites can make a lot of sense.

Freezer do's and don'ts

The freezer preserves food by keeping it frozen at a temperature of –18°C/0°F or less, which reduces chemical changes and renders micro-organisms inactive. If used properly, your freezer will stock food that is indistinguishable from fresh in terms of colour, texture and flavour. Bear the following tips in mind to ensure you get the most from your freezer:

Do

- cool food quickly and freeze only when quite cold
- remove surplus fat (see Meat, page 10)
- pack food for the freezer carefully and seal securely, removing excess air and leaving **headspace** (a gap between the surface of the food and the lid or cover) where indicated, especially for liquids, to allow for expansion
- freeze food as fast as possible to avoid the formation of large ice crystals and ensure that the food retains its original texture: all freezers have a **fast-freeze** switch, and some have a special fast-freezing compartment
- rotate foods in the freezer so nothing gets forgotten
- stick to recommended storage times
- follow directions for thawing carefully

Don't

- put strain on the appliance by freezing too much at one time
- buy too much of any single item, however much of a bargain it seems at the time, if it robs you of space
- forget to defrost your freezer from time to time
- freeze fresh fish unless 100 per cent sure it's absolutely fresh.

The recipes and charts in this book give a good idea of what you *can* freeze well. There are some items it's unwise or unnecessary to freeze and a few that simply won't.

- The unfreezables are: avocado pears (although an avocado mousse or dip will freeze), boiled old potatoes, cottage cheese or cream cheese, sour cream (unless made up into quiches, cheesecakes, etc), yoghurt (unless commercially frozen), single or unwhipped whipping cream, custards, whole raw or hard-boiled eggs (although raw egg white will freeze), brittle icings, mayonnaise, salad greens and soft meringue.

Packing

Basically, packaging must efficiently protect the food from direct contact with the very cold air of the freezer, which causes dehydration and **'freezer burn'** – brown or whitish patches on the surface of frozen food. It must also be moisture-proof, and must eliminate as much air as possible to avoid deterioration and rancidity.

You'll be able to freeze most of the recipes in this book using:

- a supply of ordinary cling film; heavy duty foil; heavy duty polythene bags; foil dishes and rigid plastic containers such as scrupulously clean empty margarine tubs and yoghurt pots, as well as special containers with snap-on lids.

Specially laminated heavy duty foil bags are a useful alternative to rigid containers, for soups, sauces, casseroles, etc. When filled they have a box shape which makes them easy to stack and saves on freezer space.

A useful tip is to **block freeze:** line a casserole dish with foil before the food is added, then freeze the cooked food in the dish. Once frozen remove the solid foil package, wrap and seal. The food can be returned to the same dish for reheating and serving.

Labelling is essential. The name of the food or recipe, the vital use-by date, number of servings and reheating instructions should always be clearly marked.

Vegetables

Most vegetables freeze well, with the exception of salad greens. Tomatoes and onions lose firmness when frozen but can be used in stews and sauces.

Don't waste space on vegetables you can readily and cheaply obtain fresh, or if the preparation is labour-intensive.

Select young, tender, unblemished vegetables for the freezer, and prepare them as for everyday cooking. Most vegetables require **blanching** in boiling water before freezing, to stop the enzymes working and retain the original colour and flavour. This is best done in a blanching basket which is lowered into boiling water for the required time (see chart). The vegetables are then plunged into iced water, drained and thoroughly dried before freezing.

The **open-freeze** process is used for most vegetables, to keep them separate and prevent them becoming mushy when they are stored in a container. Lay the blanched vegetables in a single layer on baking sheets or trays, place in the freezer until solid, then pack into polythene bags or rigid containers, leaving 1 cm (½ inch) headspace.

To serve, all frozen vegetables should be cooked from frozen in the minimum of boiling salted water, unless otherwise stated. Take care not to overcook.

• A selection of the wide range of vegetables suitable for freezing

SIX OF THE BEST			
Vegetable	**Packaging**	**Serving**	**Storage Time**
Beans, broad French and runner	Blanch for 2 minutes, open freeze. Pack in polythene bags, seal and label	Cook in boiling salted water, 5-10 minutes	Up to 1 year
Broccoli Brussels Sprouts	Blanch for 3-4 minutes, open freeze. Pack in rigid containers with headspace, seal and label	Cook in boiling salted water, 5-8 minutes	Up to 1 year
Carrots	Freeze baby carrots whole, large ones sliced. Blanch for 2 minutes, open freeze. Pack as for Beans	Cook in boiling salted water for 5-10 minutes	Up to 1 year
Cauliflower	Blanch florets for 3 minutes, open freeze, pack as Sprouts	Cook for 4-6 minutes. Best served with a sauce	Up to 6 months
Corn on the cob	Blanch small cobs for 4 minutes, medium for 6. Open freeze, pack in polythene bags, seal and label	Thaw for 2 hours at room temperature. Cook in boiling unsalted water for 12-15 minutes.	Up to 1 year
Courgettes	Blanch small, young courgettes for 1 minute, open freeze, pack as Broccoli. Or slice large courgettes, blanch for 2 minutes. Pack as above	Cook whole in boiling salted water for 3 minutes, thaw slices for 2 hours at room temperature and sauté in butter	Up to 1 year

Fruit

Freezing fruit involves marginally more techniques than freezing vegetables, since the range of textures is greater.

Many fruits can be prepared by the open-freeze technique (see page 5), especially if they are to be used in pies or tarts. You may need to dip the slices or sections first in water, to which lemon juice or ascorbic acid (available from chemists – 500 mg is required for every 600 ml (1 pint) water) has been added to prevent discolouration – this applies particularly to apples, pears and peaches.

Peel the fruit or, in the case of peaches and apricots, blanch in boiling water and rub off the skins. Remove stones or cores and slice directly into acidulated water. Dry the fruit thoroughly before open-freezing.

Fruit keeps longer in the freezer if packed in sugar or sugar syrup.

There are four basic methods for preparing fruit for the freezer:

Free flow pack: Open-freeze, then pack in rigid containers or polythene bags.

Dry sugar pack: Open-freeze, then pack in sugar. When the fruit is thawed, the sugar combines with the fruit juice to form a syrup. This method is particularly good for whole or sliced soft, juicy fruit. As a guide, about 450 g (1 lb) caster sugar is needed per 2 kg (4 lb) of fruit.

Sugar syrup: There are three strengths of syrup: heavy, medium and light. Medium strength is most often used but you may need a light syrup for fruits with delicate flavours. Heavy sugar syrup is suitable for tart-flavoured fruit that is not especially juicy, such as apricots or pears. Make the syrup by dissolving the sugar in the water and cool completely before using. The basic quantity of water required is 1.2 litres (2 pints). For light syrup add 225 g (8 oz) sugar, for medium 450 g (1 lb) and for heavy add 1 kg (2 lb) sugar.

Purée: Fruit purées freeze very well and are versatile. They can be used in pies, tarts, sauces, puddings and some cakes. Purée the fruit (lightly cooked if necessary) in a blender or food processor, or press through a sieve, and add sugar to taste. 50-100 g (2-4 oz) sugar is needed for every 450 g (1 lb) of fruit. Pack in rigid containers (block freeze to save containers), allowing 1 cm (½ inch) headspace.

• A variety of fruits at several different stages of the freezing process

SIX OF THE BEST			
Fruit	**Packaging**	**Serving**	**Storage Time**
Apples	Slice into acidulated water, dry. Free flow freeze or pack in light syrup or freeze as purée or sauce (page 63)	Thaw in wrappings for 2-3 hours at room temperature. Use sliced fruit in puddings; thaw purée or sauce as per recipe	Free flow pack or syrup – 1 year. Purée or sauce – 6 months
BERRIES: strawberries, raspberries, blackberries, etc	Free flow or dry sugar pack or pack in medium syrup	Leave in wrappings for 2-3 hours at room temperature. Use just before thawed	Up to 1 year
CITRUS FRUITS: oranges, lemons, grapefruit	Freeze whole, tightly wrapped in polythene, or sliced	Thaw in wrappings for 3-4 hours. Use as required	Up to 1 year
CURRANTS: blackcurrants freeze best	Free flow or dry sugar pack or pack in light syrup	Thaw in wrappings for 3 hours at room temperature	Up to 1 year
Gooseberries	Free flow or pack in medium syrup or freeze as cooked purée	Thaw in wrappings for 3 hours at room temperature, purée overnight in the refrigerator	Up to 1 year
Rhubarb	Blanch for 1 minute, free flow pack	Thaw in wrappings for 4 hours at room temperature, add sugar	Up to 1 year

Meat

It is very convenient to have a good supply of meat in the freezer to suit your personal requirements. A large family may benefit from a bulk purchase, such as a whole lamb, half a pig, a fore or hindquarter of beef, but it is pointless to buy vast quantities of one type of meat if you're not going to enjoy *all* of it. Most butchers will freeze meat for you. Check supermarket deep-freeze cabinets regularly for different cuts of frozen meat, and look for good bulk buys from freezer centres.

It is important when freezing meat to trim off excess fat. Not only does this take up unnecessary space in the freezer, but it actually shortens freezer life because it does not last as long.

Prepare the freezer by switching to fast freeze at least 2 hours before starting to freeze a bulk purchase. This reduces the risk of the temperature rising when a large amount of meat is added at one time. It also helps if you freeze relatively small loads each time, keeping the meat waiting to be frozen in your refrigerator or even leaving it with your butcher, stored in his freezer, until you are ready for it.

Fresh meat must be thoroughly wrapped before being frozen. Any surface directly exposed to the intense cold of the freezer will rapidly dehydrate and deteriorate (called freezer burn). Wrap joints in double duty foil (padding sharp bones with small pieces of foil) or wrap in cling film and overwrap in heavy-duty polythene bags. Press out as much air as possible. Small cuts (chops, steaks, etc) should be separated with freezer paper or foil to ensure easy removal before overwrapping in foil or polythene bags. Mark packages carefully, different coloured labels for different types of meat are a good idea, and be sure to mark the use-by date.

Freeze offal, mince, sausages and diced stewing meat first, placing each package directly on the fast-freeze shelf of an upright model or against the base or sides of a chest freezer. Large joints should be frozen last and you should keep the appliance at fast-freeze for about 12 hours after adding the final batch of meat.

FREEZING AND THAWING FRESH MEAT		
Type	**Storage life**	**Thawing times**
BEEF Large joints – over 1.5 kg (3¼ lb) in weight	12 months	Preferably thaw before cooking: Allow 6-7 hours per 450 g (1 lb) in the refrigerator or 2-3 hours per 450 g (1 lb) at room temperature
Small joints – under 1.5 kg (3¼ lb)	6 months	Preferably thaw before cooking: Allow 3-4 hours per 450 g (1 lb) in the refrigerator or 1-2 hours per 450 g (1 lb) at room temperature
Steaks, chops, stewing steak	6 months	Can be cooked from frozen but it may be easier to thaw first for 5-6 hours in the refrigerator or 2-4 hours at room temperature
LAMB Large joints	9 months	As beef
Small joints	6 months	As beef
Leg steaks, chops, cutlets	6 months	As beef
PORK AND VEAL Large joints	6 months	As beef
Small joints	3 months	As beef
Fillet, chops Sliced belly	3 months	As beef
Bacon joints	Smoked 2 months Unsmoked 1 month	Thaw overnight in the refrigerator. Soak if required before cooking in usual way
Bacon rashers, chops, gammon steaks	Smoked 2 months Unsmoked 2-3 weeks	Cook from frozen
OFFAL, MINCE AND SAUSAGES All types	2-3 months	Thaw before cooking: 5-6 hours in the refrigerator; 2-4 hours at room temperature
COOKED MEAT DISHES See individual recipes	See individual recipes	See individual recipes

- **A large number of different cuts of meat take well to freezing**

Poultry and game

All fresh poultry must be thoroughly cleaned before being frozen. Truss whole birds, then wrap in foil and over-wrap in a heavy-duty polythene bag. Remove as much air as possible, seal and label. Never stuff a bird before freezing – freeze stuffing separately. Giblets may also be frozen separately but for only 2-3 months.

Chicken joints or portions should be wrapped individually or interleaved with foil or freezer paper.

All poultry *must* be thoroughly thawed before cooking.

Game birds such as pheasant and partridge may be treated like chicken, but should be hung before freezing to achieve the desired flavour. Do not lard venison before freezing. Rabbit should be completely fresh, skinned and cleaned, frozen either whole or in joints.

FREEZING AND THAWING POULTRY AND GAME		
Type	**Storage life**	**Thawing times**
Chicken – up to 2 kg (4 lb)	9 months	Thaw in refrigerator for 15-20 hours (5 hours per 450 g/1 lb), or for 3-4 hours per 450 g/(1 lb) at room temperature
Chicken over 2 kg (4½ lb)	9 months	Thaw in refrigerator for 24-36 hours (6 hours per 450 g/1 lb) or for 4-5 hours per 450 g (1 lb) at room temperature
Duck and Goose	6 months	As for chicken over 2 kg (4½ lb)
Turkey – up to 6 kg (13 lb)	6 months	Thaw in refrigerator for 65-70 hours or 20-24 hours at room temperature
Over 6 kg (13 lb)	6 months	Thaw in refrigerator for 75-96 hours or for 30-48 hours at room temperature
Game, Hare, Rabbit	6 months	Thaw in refrigerator for 6 hours per 450 g (1 lb) or for 3 hours per 450 g (1 lb) at room temperature

• **Frozen stock will help you produce quick sauces for frozen poultry or game**

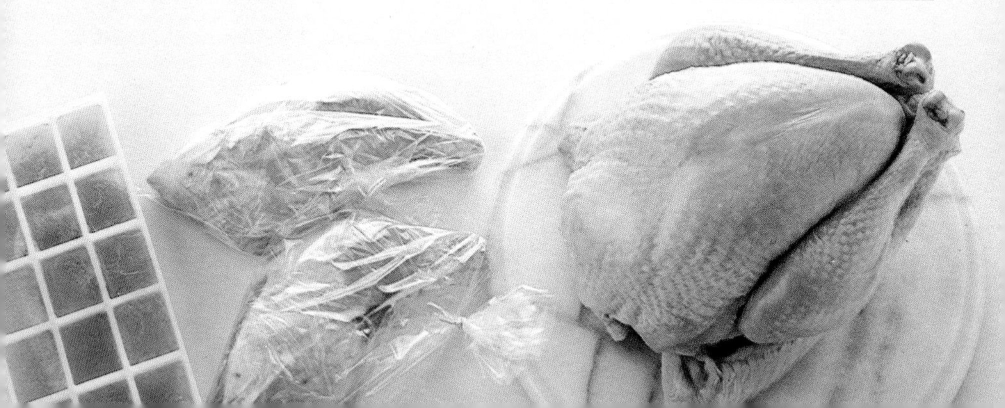

• The ability to freeze breads and cakes adds a new dimension to your home baking

Baked goods

All baked goods freeze extremely well. Cakes, breads and scones are best baked before freezing whereas pastry dough will be crisper if frozen before baking.

Bread loves the freezer. You can freeze cooked loaves or rolls (white is better than brown, which may be crumbly on thawing), or unrisen dough (for which you will require one and a half times the amount of yeast specified in any bread recipe). Yeast products dehydrate readily in the freezer, so wrap breads, rolls, etc. very carefully. It is safest to wrap them in cling film and then overwrap in a plastic bag.

As a general rule it is best to freeze cakes before icing, placing a piece of freezer paper or polythene between layers to keep them apart. However, it is useful to have a few iced cakes on hand for unexpected guests, so use butter-cream to fill and top these if possible, and open-freeze before wrapping. Slice some cakes before freezing – individually wrapped slices can then be taken from the freezer as required, and a single slice thaws much faster than a slab of cake.

Biscuits, both baked and unbaked, can be frozen. Uncooked biscuit dough may be conveniently frozen in a cylinder shape, then thawed slightly before the biscuit rounds are sliced off and baked.

BAKED GOODS			
Item	**Packaging**	**Serving**	**Storage Time**
Baked bread, soft rolls, croissants	Wrap in cling-film or foil. Overwrap in a polythene bag. Seal and label. Freeze	Thaw in wrappings for 2-4 hours at room temperature or, if wrapped in foil, reheat from frozen in a 200°C, 400°F, Gas Mark 6 oven	6 months
Crusty bread and rolls	As above	As above	1 week
Tea breads	As above	As above	3 months
Bread dough, unrisen	Pack into a greased polythene bag, leave 2.5-5 cm (1-2 inches) of space above the dough and seal the bag with a fastener. Label and freeze	Remove the fastener. Thaw and rise in the refrigerator overnight or for 2-3 hours at room temperature. Knead and shape before baking	2 weeks
Breadcrumbs	Pack in polythene bags, seal, label and freeze	Thaw in wrappings for 1-2 hours at room temperature	2-3 months
Sandwiches	Wrap tightly in cling film, keeping different flavours apart and overwrap in a polythene bag. Seal, label, freeze	Thaw in wrappings for 2-3 hours at room temperature	1-2 months
Uncooked cake mixtures	Transfer to polythene containers, seal, label and freeze	Thaw for 2-3 hours at room temperature, then bake in greased tins in usual way	1 month
Baked cakes, plain	Wrap in foil or polythene bags, exclude as much air as possible, seal, label and freeze	Thaw in wrappings for 3-5 hours at room temperature	4 months
Cakes, decorated	Open freeze, then wrap carefully in cling film, overwrap in a polythene bag, seal, label and return to the freezer	Remove wrappings and thaw for 2-4 hours at room temperature	3 months

Item	Packaging	Serving	Storage Time
Biscuits, unbaked	Wrap dough in loaf or cylinder shape in cling film, overwrap in a polythene bag, seal, label and freeze. If biscuits are shaped with a cutter, open freeze on baking sheets, wrap in cling film and overwrap in foil or pack into rigid containers, seal, label and freeze	If in loaf form, thaw only until slices can be cut off for baking. If in cut form, cook from frozen, after unwrapping	6 months
Scones, cooked	Place cold scones in polythene bags, seal, label and freeze	Reheat from frozen in a 180°C, 350°F, Gas Mark 4 oven for 15-20 minutes	6 months
Cheesecakes	Open freeze, wrap in foil, seal, label and freeze	Unwrap, then thaw in the refrigerator overnight or for 4-5 hours at room temperature	1 month
Pastry, uncooked	Form into rectangular blocks, wrap in cling film, overwrap in a polythene bag, label and freeze or shape as required. Open freeze in tins, then remove frozen pastry shells and pack in rigid containers. Seal, label, freeze again	Remove wrappings and thaw at room temperature for 1 hour. Prick pastry after thawing and bake as usual	3 months
Cooked pies	Bake pies in foil dishes, cool quickly, wrap in foil, seal, label and freeze	Thaw for 2-4 hours at room temperature or reheat from frozen in a 180°C, 350°F, Gas Mark 4 oven	2 months
Open flans or tarts, filled	Open freeze until solid, wrap in foil or place in a polythene bag, seal, label and return to freezer	Unwrap and thaw for 3 hours at room temperature	2 months

SOUPS AND STARTERS

Minestrone

SERVES 8

2 tbls olive oil
3 rashers streaky bacon, rinded and diced
2 onions, chopped
2 carrots, sliced
1 small potato, diced
2 celery stalks, sliced
2 leeks, sliced
3 large tomatoes, skinned, seeded and chopped
100 g (4 oz) French beans
100 g (4 oz) haricot beans, soaked overnight, drained
2 tbls tomato purée
1 tsp dried basil
2 tsp chopped fresh parsley
1 litre (1¾ pints) Chicken stock (see page 60)
salt and pepper
25 g (1 oz) shortcut macaroni
grated Parmesan cheese, to serve

Heat the oil in a large saucepan, add the bacon and fry for 2-3 minutes, until the fat runs. Add the onions, carrots, potato, celery, leeks, tomatoes and the French beans. Cover and cook gently, stirring occasionally, for 5 minutes.

Add the haricot beans, tomato purée and herbs. Stir in the stock, season to taste and bring to the boil. Cover the pan again, reduce the heat and simmer for 50 minutes, stirring occasionally.

Add the pasta and simmer for a further 10 minutes or until tender.

To freeze: Cool quickly and pour the soup into rigid containers, in one-portion quantities if desired. Cover, seal, label and freeze for up to 6 weeks with bacon. Without the bacon, the soup will freeze for up to 3 months.
To serve: Turn into a large saucepan, add 2 tbls water and reheat gently for about 1 hour, stirring and turning the block occasionally. Adjust seasoning to taste. Serve the soup with grated Parmesan cheese and crusty bread.
Variations: Vegetarians could omit the bacon and substitute vegetable stock for the chicken stock. If liked, 1 tsp yeast extract could be added for extra flavour.

Ham and pea soup

SERVES 8

500 g (1¼ lb) dried split peas, soaked overnight, drained
1 large knuckle bacon, soaked overnight, drained
1 onion, finely chopped
2 celery stalks, finely chopped
1 potato, diced
2.75 litres (5 pints) water
pepper

Place the split peas in a large saucepan with the knuckle of bacon. Add the onion, celery, potato and water.

Bring to the boil, then reduce the heat, cover and simmer for 3 hours. Remove from the heat and remove the bacon from the pan. Dice the meat, discarding fat and bone, and return to the soup. Adjust seasoning to taste.

To freeze: Cool quickly and pour the soup into rigid containers. Cover, seal, label and freeze for up to 6 weeks.
To serve: Turn into a large saucepan, add 2 tbls water and reheat gently for about 1 hour, stirring and turning the block occasionally. Adjust seasoning to taste. Serve garnished with croûtons.
Variation: For an even more substantial meal, add sliced frankfurters to the soup just before the end of cooking.

Asparagus cheese soup

SERVES 6

25g (1 oz) butter
1 small onion, chopped
750g (1½ lb) fresh asparagus, cut into 2.5cm (1 inch) pieces
1.2 litres (2 pints) well-flavoured chicken stock (page 60)
salt and white pepper
100g (4 oz) Brie or Camembert cheese, diced
a few drops of green food colouring (optional)
To garnish
142 ml (5 fl oz) carton single cream
a few cooked asparagus spears

Melt the butter in a large saucepan, add the onion and cook gently for 5 minutes, until soft and lightly coloured. Add the asparagus and cook for a further 1-2 minutes. Pour in the stock, season to taste and bring to the boil. Cover, reduce the heat and simmer for about 25 minutes, or until the asparagus is tender.

Remove from the heat. Purée the soup in a blender or food processor. Add the diced cheese and process again until smooth. Adjust seasoning to taste and add food colouring if liked.

To freeze: Cool quickly and pour the soup into rigid containers, in one-portion quantities if desired. Cover, seal, label and freeze for up to 1 month.
To serve: Thaw at room temperature for 3-4 hours. Reheat gently in a large saucepan for 15 minutes, then bring to the boil, stirring frequently. Adjust seasoning to taste. Serve garnished with cream and asparagus spears.

• **From left to right: Minestrone; Ham and pea soup; Asparagus cheese soup**

Mediterranean fish soup

SERVES 6

50g (2oz) butter
2 onions, sliced
1 garlic clove, crushed
2 leeks, sliced into rings
1 tbls tomato purée
2 potatoes, sliced
397g (14oz) can tomatoes
finely grated rind of ½ lemon
600ml (1 pint) Chicken stock (see page 60)
1 bouquet garni
salt and pepper
100g (4oz) haddock fillet, skinned and cut into 2.5cm (1 inch) cubes
100g (4oz) cod fillet, skinned and cut into 2.5cm (1 inch) cubes
2 tbls dry white wine
100g (4oz) peeled prawns
chopped fresh thyme, to garnish

Melt the butter in a large saucepan, add the onions, garlic and leeks, cover and cook gently for 5 minutes over very low heat, stirring frequently.

Add the tomato purée, potatoes, tomatoes with their juice, lemon rind, stock, bouquet garni and salt and pepper to taste. Cover and simmer for 15 minutes. Add the haddock and cod to the saucepan with the wine. Cook over moderate heat for 5 minutes, then add the prawns. Reduce the heat, cover and simmer for 10-15 minutes or until the fish is tender, stirring occasionally.

To freeze: Cool quickly and pour the soup into rigid containers. Cover, seal, label and freeze for up to 1 month.
To serve: Turn into a large saucepan, add 2 tbls water and reheat gently for about 1 hour, stirring and turning the block occasionally. Adjust seasoning to taste and serve sprinkled with thyme, accompanied by crusty bread.
Variation: For a special occasion, serve the soup in a heated tureen, garnished with 75g (3oz) prawns in their shells. Hook the prawns over the sides of the tureen for a colourful effect.

French country pâté

SERVES 8-10

1 tsp vegetable oil
8 rashers streaky bacon, rinded
450g (1 lb) pig's liver
450g (1 lb) chicken livers
225g (8oz) belly of pork
175g (6oz) fresh white breadcrumbs
2 eggs, beaten
2 garlic cloves, crushed with ½ tsp salt
85ml (3fl oz) red wine
2 tbls brandy (optional)
2 tsp chopped fresh thyme or 1 tsp dried
50g (2oz) blanched almonds, coarsely chopped
pepper
parsley sprigs, to garnish

Heat the oven to 160°C, 325°F, Gas Mark 3. Brush a 1 kg/2 lb loaf tin with the oil. Lay the bacon rashers on a board and stretch them with the blade of a knife, then use to line the base and sides of the tin. Set aside.

Mince together the pig's liver, chicken livers and pork, then place in a large bowl. Add the remaining ingredients with pepper to taste and stir to mix.

Spoon into the prepared tin and level the surface. Cover with foil, then stand the tin in a roasting pan. Pour in boiling water to come halfway up sides of tin. Bake in the oven for 2½ hours until the pâté has shrunk from the sides of the tin and the juices run slightly pink when a skewer is inserted into the pâté.

Drain off the excess fat and leave to cool completely.

• Mediterranean fish soup
French country pâté

To freeze: Cool quickly, then run a knife blade around the edge of the pâté and turn out on to a piece of heavy duty foil. Wrap securely, then place in a polythene bag, seal, label and freeze for up to 2 weeks.
To serve: Thaw in the refrigerator overnight. Serve the pâté chilled, cut into thick slices and garnished with parsley. Chunks of French bread or wholemeal toast go well with this pâté.
Variation: For a gamey flavour, omit the thyme and almonds and substitute 8 crushed allspice or juniper berries and 1 teaspoon mustard powder.

Crab vol au vents

SERVES 4-6

370 g (13 oz) frozen puff pastry, thawed
198 g (7 oz) can crabmeat, drained and flaked
92 g (3¼ oz) can peeled prawns, drained
1 tsp lemon juice
300 ml (½ pint) Béchamel sauce (see page 61)
2 tbls dry sherry
½ tsp French mustard
½ tsp dried mixed herbs
salt and pepper
2 tbls double cream
1 egg, beaten, to glaze
whole prawns and dill springs, to garnish

Roll the pastry out to 5 mm (¼ inch) thickness on a floured board. Using a 9 cm (3½ inch) pastry cutter, cut 6 pastry circles and place on a dampened baking tray. Using a 5 cm (2 inch) pastry cutter, cut halfway through each circle. Set aside.

In a bowl, combine the crabmeat, prawns and lemon juice. Mix together lightly.

Simmer the Béchamel sauce for 2 minutes, then stir in the sherry, mustard, herbs and salt and pepper to taste.

Remove from the heat and fold in the cream and the crabmeat mixture. Cover the surface of the crabmeat sauce with cling film to prevent a skin forming.

To freeze: **Pastry cases:** open freeze until solid, then pack in a rigid container. Cover, seal, label and freeze for up to 3 months.

Crabmeat filling: cool the mixture quickly, then remove the cling film and transfer the filling to a rigid container. Cover, seal, label and freeze. Store for up to 3 months.

To serve: Heat the oven to 220°C, 425°F, Gas Mark 7.

Unwrap pastry cases, brush with the beaten egg and thaw at room temperature for 30 minutes. Bake in the centre of the oven for 20 minutes or until well risen and crisp. Allow to cool. Using a sharp knife, carefully remove the pastry lids and reserve.

Meanwhile turn the filling into a large saucepan and reheat very gently for about 30 minutes, stirring and turning the block occasionally. When fully thawed, increase the heat and cook for 10 minutes, but do not allow the mixture to boil. Adjust seasoning to taste. Spoon the mixture into the vol au vents, replace the lids and serve, garnished with prawns and dill.

Tomato and anchovy tarts

SERVES 5

For the pastry
225 g (8 oz) wholemeal flour
½ tsp salt
50 g (2 oz) lard, diced
50 g (2 oz) margarine or butter, diced
cold water to mix
For the filling
3 tbls olive oil
3 large onions, thinly sliced
6 tomatoes, skinned and roughly chopped
1 garlic clove, crushed
1 tsp dried mixed herbs
salt and pepper
56 g (2 oz) can anchovy fillets, drained and soaked in 2 tbls milk for 15 minutes, rinsed and dried
10 black olives, stoned
basil sprigs, to garnish

Heat the oven to 180°C, 350°F, Gas Mark 4.

Sift the flour with the salt into a mixing bowl, add the lard and margarine and rub in with the fingertips until the mixture resembles fine breadcrumbs. Add just enough water to bind to a stiff dough. Knead lightly until smooth.

Turn the dough on to a floured board, roll out to 5 mm/¼ inch thickness, and use to line 10 × 7.5 cm (3 inch) tartlet tins. Prick the pastry with a fork and chill for 20 minutes.

Meanwhile prepare the filling. Heat the oil in a saucepan, add the onions and fry over low heat for about 5 minutes, until soft and lightly coloured. Stir in the tomatoes, garlic and herbs and cook, uncovered, for 15 minutes, until the sauce is thick. Season to taste and set aside.

Line the tartlet cases with foil and fill with baking beans. Bake blind in the oven for 7 minutes. Remove the foil and beans. Spoon the tomato filling into the tartlet cases. Arrange the anchovy fillets in a lattice design over the top and top with the olives.

Bake for 10 minutes, then remove from the oven and allow the tartlets to cool in the tins for 10 minutes. Transfer to a wire rack to cool completely.

To freeze: Open freeze the tartlets until solid. Pack in a rigid container, seal, label and freeze for up to 4 months.
To serve: Remove the tartlets from the container and place on a wire rack. Thaw at room temperature for 2 hours. Serve cold, garnished with basil, or reheat in a 180°C, 350°F, Gas Mark 4 oven for 7-10 minutes.

• Crab vol au vents; Tomato and anchovy tarts

Beef with green peppercorns

SERVES 4

2 tbls vegetable oil
1 kg (2 lb) chuck steak, trimmed and cut into 2.5 cm (1 inch) cubes
1 large onion, chopped
2-3 celery stalks, chopped
1 garlic clove, crushed with 1 tsp salt
4 rashers streaky bacon, rinded and chopped
3 tbls green peppercorns, drained
3 tbls chopped fresh parsley
2 bay leaves
salt
300 ml (½ pint) dry white wine
150 ml (¼ pint) Beef stock (see page 60)

Heat the oven to 160°C, 325°F, Gas Mark 3.

Heat the oil in a large flameproof casserole, add the meat cubes and fry over moderately high heat, stirring and turning, for about 5 minutes, to seal and brown on all sides. Remove the beef with a slotted spoon and drain on absorbent kitchen paper.

Add the onion, celery, garlic and bacon to the casserole. Fry over moderate heat, stirring constantly, for about 4-5 minutes, until soft. Crush 2 tbls of the peppercorns in a mortar with a pestle, then mix them with 2 tbls of the parsley. Stir the mixture into the casserole with the bay leaves and salt to taste.

Return the meat to the casserole. Stir in the wine and stock and bring to the boil over moderately high heat. Cover tightly and cook in the oven for 1½-2 hours, or until the meat is tender. Remove from the oven, discard the bay leaves, and add the remaining peppercorns and parsley.

To freeze: Cool quickly, tranfer to a foil container, cover, seal, label and freeze for up to 6 weeks.

To serve: Thaw overnight in the refrigerator. Stir, then reheat in a casserole in a 180°C, 350°F, Gas Mark 4 oven for 30-45 minutes, or until piping hot. Serve with new potatoes and a green vegetable such as whole green beans.

Steak and kidney pie

SERVES 6

50 g (2 oz) dripping or lard
2 large onions, sliced
1 kg (2 lb) lean stewing beef, trimmed and cut into 2.5 cm (1 inch) cubes
225 g (8 oz) kidney, cores removed and cut into bite-sized pieces
50 g (2 oz) plain flour
225 g (8 oz) mushrooms, thickly sliced
300 ml (½ pint) Beef stock (see page 60)
½ tsp dried marjoram
1 bay leaf
salt and pepper
215 g (7½ oz) frozen puff pastry, thawed
1 egg, beaten, to glaze

Melt the dripping in a heavy saucepan, add the onions and fry gently for 2-3 minutes or until transparent. Toss the steak and kidney in the flour, shake off and reserve the excess. Add the meat to the pan and fry briskly for about 5 minutes, turning, to seal and brown on all sides.

Add the mushrooms to the pan and sprinkle in any reserved flour. Cook for 1 minute, stirring, then gradually stir in the stock, marjoram, bay leaf and salt and pepper to taste.

Bring to the boil, stirring constantly, then reduce heat, cover and simmer for

1-2 hours, or until the meat is tender.

Discard the bay leaf, turn the meat into a foil pie dish and allow to cool.

Roll out the pastry to a 5 mm/¼ inch thickness on a floured board. Cut a narrow strip long enough to go round the edge of the pie dish. Dampen the edge of the pie dish with water and press the strip in place. Brush with more water. Cover the meat with the remaining pastry and press down to seal then trim, knock up and flute Score the top of the pie in a trellis pattern with a sharp knife. Make a small hole in the top of the pie to allow the steam to escape.

• Beef with green peppercorns
Steak and kidney pie

To freeze: Wrap the pie in foil, seal, label and freeze for up to 4 weeks.

To serve: Unwrap the pie and brush the pastry with egg to glaze. Place the pie in a 220°C, 425°F, Gas Mark 7 oven for 30 minutes. Reduce the heat to 180°C, 350°F, Gas Mark 4, and bake for a further 30 minutes. If the pastry shows signs of overbrowning, cover with foil. Serve with young carrots and broccoli.

• Pork with lemon and lime; Basque-style chicken breasts

Pork with lemon and lime

SERVES 4

25g (1 oz) margarine or butter
1 garlic clove, crushed
2 onions, chopped
450g (1 lb) leg of pork, cut into 1 cm (½ inch) pieces
finely grated rind of 1 lemon
2 tbls fresh lime juice
150 ml (¼ pint) water
salt and pepper
To finish
2 tbls single cream
1 egg yolk
grated lemon or lime zest
lemon or lime slices

Heat the oven to 190°C, 375°F, Gas Mark 5.

Melt the margarine in a large frying pan, add the garlic and onions and fry for 2-3 minutes, until transparent. Using a slotted spoon, transfer the vegetables to a medium flameproof casserole. Add the pork to the fat remaining in the frying pan and fry over moderate heat for about 3 minutes, turning frequently. Add the pork to the casserole with the lemon rind, lime juice, water and salt and pepper to taste.

Cover the casserole, and bake for 40 minutes, or until the pork is tender.

To freeze: Cool quickly, transfer to a foil container, cover, seal, label and freeze for up to 6 weeks.
To serve: Thaw overnight in the refrigerator. Stir, then reheat in a 180°C, 350°F, Gas Mark 4 oven for 30 minutes. Transfer the pork to a serving dish and keep hot. Mix the cream with the egg yolk, season well and add a little sauce from the casserole. Beat lightly, stir the cream mixture back into the sauce and pour into a saucepan. Cook over low heat, stirring constantly, until the sauce thickens, but do not allow to boil. Pour the sauce over the pork and garnish with lemon slices and grated zest.

Basque-style chicken breasts

SERVES 4

4 tbls olive oil
4 chicken breasts, skinned
1 onion, finely chopped
1 garlic clove, crushed with ½ tsp salt
1 red pepper, cored, seeded and cut into rings
1 green pepper, cored, seeded and cut into rings
397 g (14 oz) can tomatoes
1 tbls tomato purée
150 ml (¼ pint) Chicken stock (see page 60)
4 tbls brandy
2 tsp chopped fresh rosemary or 1 tsp dried
2 tsp chopped fresh thyme or 1 tsp dried
salt and pepper

Heat the oil in a large flameproof casserole, add the chicken breasts and fry over moderate heat, turning the pieces frequently, for 5-7 minutes to brown on all sides. Remove the chicken and set aside on a plate. Cover loosely.

Add the onion to the oil remaining in the casserole and fry gently for 2-3 minutes, until transparent.

Add the garlic and the red and green peppers and fry for a further 2-3 minutes, then stir in the tomatoes with their juice, tomato purée, chicken stock and brandy. Bring to the boil.

Reduce the heat, add the herbs and salt and pepper to taste, then return the chicken to the pan. Simmer gently, uncovered, for 45 minutes, or until the chicken is tender and the sauce is reduced.

To freeze: Cool quickly, transfer to a foil container, cover, seal, label and freeze for up to 2 months.
To serve: Thaw overnight in the refrigerator. Stir, then reheat in a casserole in a 180°C, 350°F, Gas Mark 4 oven for 45 minutes to 1 hour. Serve with rice or boiled new potatoes and a simple chicory salad.
Variation: Pork fillet may be substituted for the chicken. You will require 2 fillets, about 350 g (12 oz) each, trimmed and halved.

Stuffed breast of lamb

SERVES 4

100 g (4 oz) pork sausagemeat
1 egg, beaten
4 slices white bread, crusts removed and crumbed
1 tsp dried mixed herbs
1 tsp French mustard
salt and pepper
2 breasts of lamb, boned and trimmed
1 large potato, diced
2 carrots, sliced
1 parsnip, diced
1 turnip, diced
1 onion, chopped
2 tbls plain flour
300 ml (½ pint) Beef stock (see page 60)
2 tbls chopped fresh parsley, to garnish

Heat the oven to 160°C, 325°F, Gas Mark 3.

In a large bowl, mix together the sausagemeat, egg, breadcrumbs, herbs, mustard and salt and pepper to taste. Spread the mixture evenly over the lamb breasts. Roll each breast up and tie in several places with string.

Place all the vegetables in a large roasting tin and sprinkle with the flour and salt and pepper. Pour in the stock. Lay the rolled breasts on top.

Cover with foil and cook in the oven for 2 hours, or until the lamb is tender and cooked through.

To freeze: Cool quickly, then wrap the stuffed lamb in heavy duty foil. Place in a polythene bag, seal, label and freeze for up to 6 weeks. Pack the vegetables in a rigid freezer container and cover, seal, label and freeze with the lamb.

To serve: Thaw at room temperature for 3-4 hours. Slice the lamb thickly. To serve hot, spoon the vegetables on to an ovenproof serving dish and arrange the meat slices on top. Cover with foil and place in a 180°C, 350°F, Gas Mark 4 oven for about 30 minutes or until heated through. Garnish with parsley and serve with baked jacket potatoes, green vegetables and mint sauce.

Variation: Rosemary and garlic go particularly well with lamb. You may like to lay a few sprigs of fresh rosemary on the bed of vegetables before cooking the lamb (remove before freezing), and add 2 crushed garlic cloves with the onion.

Lamb curry

SERVES 4

4 tbls vegetable oil
1 large onion, chopped
1 garlic clove, crushed
1 cm (½ inch) piece fresh root ginger, peeled and finely chopped
50 g (2 oz) creamed coconut
2-4 tsp curry powder
600 ml (1 pint) Beef stock (see page 60)
salt and pepper
450 g (1 lb) boneless lamb, cubed
¼ tsp ground coriander
2 tbls apricot jam
coriander sprigs, to garnish

Heat half the oil in a large saucepan, add the onion and garlic and fry for 2-3 minutes or until transparent. Stir in the ginger and coconut, reduce the heat and cook gently for 2 minutes.

Stir in the curry powder, stock and salt and pepper to taste. Bring to the boil, then reduce the heat and simmer for 15 minutes.

Meanwhile, heat the remaining oil in a large frying pan. Add the lamb, season with salt, pepper and coriander, and fry for 5-6 minutes or until well browned on all sides.

Using a slotted spoon, transfer the lamb to the sauce and cook over a very low heat for about 1 hour or until tender. Stir in the jam.

To freeze: Cool quickly, transfer to a rigid container, cover, seal, label and freeze for up to 2 months.

To serve: Thaw at room temperature for 4-6 hours. Tip into a flameproof casserole and slowly bring to the boil, stirring occasionally. Adjust the seasoning to taste. Serve garnished with coriander sprigs, accompanied by rice, tomato and onion salad, and cucumber raita.

Variation: This curry sauce may also be used with chicken, prawns or eggs.

• Stuffed breast of lamb
Lamb curry

Leek and ham flan

SERVES 4

For the pastry
100g (4oz) plain flour
½tsp salt
25g (1 oz) margarine or butter, diced
25g (1 oz) lard, diced
1 tbls cold water
For the filling
25g (1 oz) butter
1 leek, finely sliced
100g (4oz) lean cooked ham, chopped
1 egg
142ml (5oz) carton single cream
salt and pepper
watercress sprigs, to garnish

Heat the oven to 220°C, 425°F, Gas Mark 7.

Sift the flour with the salt into a mixing bowl, add the fats and rub in with the fingertips until the mixture resembles fine breadcrumbs. Add the water and mix to a firm dough. Roll out on a floured board and use to line an 18cm (7 inch) plain flan ring on a baking sheet. Chill in the refrigerator for 10 minutes. Fill with greaseproof paper and baking beans and bake blind in the oven for 15 minutes. Remove from the oven and take out the beans and paper.

Meanwhile, melt the butter in a small saucepan, add the leek and cook over low heat for 2-3 minutes or until soft but not brown. Using a slotted spoon, remove the leek and arrange in the flan case with the ham.

In a bowl, whisk the egg and cream together, season with salt and pepper and pour into the flan. Reduce the oven temperature to 180°C, 350°F, Gas Mark 4, and bake the flan in the oven for 25-30 minutes, or until the filling is set.

To freeze: Cool quickly, place in a polythene bag, seal, label and freeze for up to 2 months.
To serve: Remove the flan from the bag and thaw in the refrigerator overnight, then heat through in a 180°C, 350°F, Gas Mark 4 oven for 25 minutes. Serve garnished with watercress sprigs.
Variation: For Chicken and mushroom flan, fry 75g (3oz) sliced mushrooms with the leek, and substitute cooked chicken for the ham.

Veal goulash

SERVES 4

450g (1 lb) pie veal, trimmed and cut into 2.5cm (1 inch) cubes
1 tbls plain flour
1 tbls paprika
salt and pepper
25g (1 oz) margarine
1 onion, sliced
150ml (¼ pint) stock
2 celery stalks, sliced
3 large tomatoes, skinned, seeded and chopped
1 tbls tomato purée
To garnish
1 tbls finely chopped fresh parsley

Heat the oven to 180°C, 350°F, Gas Mark 4.

Toss the veal in the flour, seasoned with paprika, salt and pepper. Melt the margarine in a large frying pan. Add the veal and the onion and fry, stirring frequently, for 5 minutes. Add the stock and bring to the boil, stirring. Add the celery, tomatoes and tomato purée and stir well to mix.

Transfer to an ovenproof casserole. Cover and cook in the oven for 1½-1¾ hours, or until tender.

To freeze: Cool quickly, transfer to a foil container, cover, seal, label and freeze for up to 2 months.
To serve: Thaw overnight in the refrigerator. Stir, then reheat in a casserole in a 180°C, 350°F, Gas Mark 4 oven for 30-45 minutes. Adjust the seasoning to taste. Sprinkle with the chopped parsley. Serve with buttered noodles or new potatoes and lightly minted peas.
Variation: Replace the celery with 2 red peppers and add 1 crushed garlic clove with the onion. Garnish with a swirl of soured cream and a dusting of paprika.

• Veal goulash; Leek and ham flan

Spicy stuffed pancakes

SERVES 4

For the pancakes
100 g (4 oz) plain flour
¼ tsp salt
1 egg
1 tbls vegetable oil
300 ml (½ pint) milk
vegetable oil, for frying
For the filling
350 g (12 oz) lean minced beef
25 g (1 oz) plain flour
¼ tsp Tabasco
¼ tsp ground ginger
salt
198 g (7 oz) can tomatoes
1 garlic clove, crushed
1 tsp Worcestershire sauce
1 tsp wine vinegar
300 ml (½ pint) Cheese sauce (see page 61)
To finish
50 g (2 oz) Cheddar cheese, grated
2 tbls chopped fresh parsley
lemon twists

To make the pancakes, sift the flour with the salt into a mixing bowl and make a well in the centre. Pour in the egg, oil and half the milk. Using a wooden spoon or wire whisk, beat the mixture, slowly incorporating the flour. Gradually blend in the remaining milk, beating well to make a smooth batter. Pour the batter into a jug.

Heat a 20 cm (8 inch) frying pan and brush with oil. Pour in about 2 tbls of the batter and tilt and rotate the pan to spread it out evenly. Cook over moderate heat for 1 minute, then toss or turn the pancake and cook the other side for 1 minute. Turn out on to a wire rack. Make 7 more pancakes in the same way.

To make the filling, place the mince in a small non-stick saucepan and cook over low heat, stirring, for 3-4 minutes, until the fat runs. Increase the heat to moderate, stir in the flour and cook for 1 minute, stirring constantly. Remove from the heat and stir in the Tabasco, ginger, salt, tomatoes with their juice, garlic, Worcestershire sauce and vinegar. Return to the heat and bring to the boil, then cover and simmer gently for 45 minutes or until cooked through. Adjust the seasoning to taste and leave to cool.

Divide the filling equally among the pancakes and roll up. Arrange the pancakes in a single layer in a shallow foil container.

Make the cheese sauce, simmer for 2 minutes, stirring, then pour over the pancakes.

To freeze: Cool quickly, cover, label and freeze for up to 2 months.
To serve: Thaw overnight in the refrigerator. Sprinkle with 50 g (2 oz) grated Cheddar cheese and bake in a 200°C, 400°F, Gas Mark 6 oven for 30 minutes, until golden brown. Sprinkle with parsley and garnish with lemon twists. Serve with a mixed salad or with a lettuce, watercress and pear salad.
Variation: Vegetarians might like to substitute cooked red kidney beans for the minced beef. Fry 2 chopped onions in 2 tbls vegetable oil, then add the flour and proceed as in the recipe, adding the beans with the tomatoes, and cooking the filling for 15-20 minutes instead of 45 minutes.

Mushroom meat loaf

SERVES 6-8

450 g (1 lb) minced pork
450 g (1 lb) lean minced beef
1 onion, finely chopped
1 garlic clove, finely chopped
225 g (8 oz) mushrooms, finely chopped
100 g (4 oz) fresh white breadcrumbs
5 tablespoons dry white wine
1 egg, lightly beaten
salt and pepper
¼ tsp grated nutmeg
142 ml (5 fl oz) carton soured cream
150 ml (¼ pint) Beef stock (see page 60)
sliced tomatoes and gherkins, to finish

• **Spicy stuffed pancakes; Mushroom meat loaf**

Heat the oven to 200°C, 400°F, Gas Mark 6.

Place the pork and beef in a mixing bowl with the onion, garlic, mushrooms and breadcrumbs. Stir well to mix. In a small bowl, beat the wine with the egg and season to taste with salt and pepper. Add the nutmeg, then stir into the meat and breadcrumbs to make a stiff mixture. Shape into a loaf and place in a large roasting pan. Pour over the soured cream and roast in the oven for 40-50 minutes, or until the meat is cooked and a light crust is formed, basting occasionally.

Remove the loaf from the pan and place in a deep foil container. Set aside. Transfer the roasting pan to the top of the stove and pour in the stock. Stir well over low heat and strain over the loaf.

To freeze: Cool quickly, cover, overwrap in heavy duty foil, label and freeze for up to 6 weeks.

To serve: If required hot, bake the meat loaf from frozen in its wrapped foil dish in a 220°C, 425°F, Gas Mark 7 oven for 20 minutes, then reduce the heat to 190°C, 375°F, Gas Mark 5 and bake for a further 30-40 minutes, or until the loaf is heated through. Slit open the foil wrappings for the last 15 minutes to crisp the top. If required cold, thaw in wrappings overnight in the refrigerator or for 5-6 hours at room temperature. Unwrap and serve on a large platter, garnished with sliced tomatoes and gherkins. Serve with crusty bread, additional soured cream handed separately, if liked, and accompanied by potato salad and coleslaw.

Plaice in cider sauce

SERVES 4

8 small plaice fillets, skinned
1 small onion, finely chopped
25 g (1 oz) margarine or butter
15 g (½ oz) cornflour
300 ml (½ pint) dry cider
1 tbls French mustard
1 tbls finely chopped parsley
pinch of soft light brown sugar
salt and pepper
parsley sprigs, to decorate

Heat the oven to 190°C, 375°F, Gas Mark 5.

Roll up the place fillets, arrange in a buttered shallow foil container and sprinkle over the onion.

Melt the margarine in a saucepan, stir in the cornflour and cook for 1 minute, stirring constantly. Gradually stir in the cider, mustard, parsley, brown sugar and seasoning. Bring to the boil, stirring constantly. Remove from the heat and pour over the fish.

Bake in the oven for 10-15 minutes, until the plaice is cooked through.

To freeze: Cool quickly, cover, seal and freeze for up to 1 month.
To serve: Unwrap and thaw at room temperature for 3 hours, then cover and reheat in a 190°C, 375°F, Gas Mark 5 oven for 1 hour, or until heated through. Adjust the seasoning to taste and garnish with parsley sprigs. Serve with new potatoes, baked tomatoes with basil and steamed courgettes.
Variation: Dry white wine may be substituted for the cider, in which case omit the mustard and brown sugar but add a squeeze of lemon juice.

Family fish pie

SERVES 4

450 g (1 lb) cod, skinned
225 g (8 oz) frozen peas
450 ml (3/4 pint) milk
40 g (1 1/2 oz) butter
40 g (1 1/2 oz) plain flour
2 tbls mayonnaise
3 hard-boiled eggs, chopped
salt and pepper
750 g (1 1/2 lb) potatoes, peeled
a little milk and butter

Place the cod in a saucepan with the peas and milk and simmer gently for 10 minutes, or until the fish flakes easily when tested with a fork.

Strain the contents of the saucepan into a jug and transfer the fish and peas from the strainer to a bowl. Flake the fish lightly and remove any bones.

Melt the butter in the rinsed out pan. Stir in the flour and cook over low heat for 1-2 minutes. Remove from the heat and gradually stir in the strained cooking liquid, then return to the heat and bring to the boil, stirring constantly. Remove from the heat and stir in the mayonnaise. Add the fish and the peas, together with the hard-boiled eggs. Season to taste with salt and pepper. Spoon into a 1.75 litre (3 pint) foil dish.

Boil the potatoes, then drain. Mash with milk and butter and season to taste with salt and pepper. Spoon or pipe the potato over the fish mixture.

To freeze: Cool quickly, cover, label and freeze for up to 1 month.
To serve: Thaw overnight in the refrigerator, then remove the covering and reheat in a 220°C, 425°F, Gas Mark 7 oven for 30-40 minutes. Garnish with parsley and sliced tomato, if liked, and serve with carrots or buttered broccoli.
Variation: Use 450 g (1 lb) smoked haddock instead of the cod.

• From left to right: Plaice in cider sauce; Family fish pie

Strawberry fool

SERVES 4

225g (8oz) strawberries, hulled
284ml (10fl oz) carton double cream
50g (2oz) caster sugar
2 tbls Cointreau
To serve
4 whole strawberries
langue de chat biscuits

Using the back of a wooden spoon, press the strawberries through a nylon sieve. In a large bowl, whisk the cream until thick but not stiff. Then fold in the sugar, strawberry purée and Cointreau. Spoon into a rigid container.

To freeze: Cover, seal, label and freeze for up to 3 months.
To serve: Thaw in the refrigerator for 2-3 hours, then spoon into individual glasses and decorate each fool with a strawberry and serve with langue de chat biscuits.
Variation: Gooseberries make a delicious fool with a delicate colour and flavour. Substitute 450ml (3/4 pint) cooked and sieved gooseberries for the strawberries and replace the Cointreau with 2 tbls gin. Extra sugar may be needed.

• Strawberry fool

Iced raspberry soufflé

• Iced raspberry soufflé

SERVES 6

450g (1 lb) raspberries, thawed if frozen
4 egg whites
225g (8 oz) caster sugar
284 ml (10fl oz) carton double cream, lightly whipped
To finish
142 ml (5fl oz) carton double cream
extra whole fresh or frozen raspberries

Place the raspberries in a blender and purée at high speed. Line a strainer with a piece of muslin and strain the raspberry purée, pushing it through with the back of a wooden spoon.

Beat the egg whites stiffly in a large bowl, then slowly beat in the sugar, 1 tablespoon at a time. Fold in the raspberry purée, then fold in the cream.

To freeze: Pour the mixture into a freezerproof bowl or soufflé dish. Open freeze until solid, then wrap in clingfilm and overwrap in foil or place in a polythene bag. Seal, label and freeze for up to 2 weeks.
To serve: Thaw in wrappings for 1 hour in the refrigerator. Unwrap and decorate with whipped cream and whole raspberries This soufflé may also be decorated with tiny meringues or ratafias arranged round the edge.
Variation: Other soft fruit may be used instead of the raspberries: strawberries, blackberries or loganberries will all give a good result. You will need about 350 ml/12 fl oz purée and, if using strawberries, 1 tbls lemon juice.

Blackberry and apple whip

SERVES 6

40 g (1½ oz) butter
225 g (8 oz) cooking apples, peeled, cored and sliced
225 g (8 oz) blackberries
75 g (3 oz) sugar
2 tbls ground rice
grated rind of 1 lemon
1 egg, separated
142 ml (5 fl oz) carton double cream, lightly whipped, to serve
12 whole blackberries, to decorate

Melt the butter in a saucepan. Add the apples and cook gently for 5-8 minutes or until soft but not coloured. Add the blackberries and cook for a further 5 minutes or until tender.

Press blackberry and apple mixture through a sieve. Return the purée to the saucepan and stir in the sugar, ground rice and lemon rind. Beat in the egg yolk and stir over very gentle heat without allowing to boil for about 5 minutes or until thickened. Remove from heat and allow to cool.

To freeze: Transfer to a rigid container, cover, seal, label and freeze for up to 6 months. Pack and freeze the egg white separately. Open freeze the whole blackberries, then pack into a small rigid container and freeze.
To serve: Thaw the purée, whole blackberries and egg white overnight in the refrigerator. Spoon the purée into 6 parfait glasses. Whisk the egg white stiffly, fold into the cream and put a spoonful on top of each glass. Chill in the refrigerator for 2-3 hours. Serve chilled, decorated with the whole blackberries.
Variation: This versatile whip may also be made with damsons, gooseberries or blackcurrants.

Orange syrup pudding

SERVES 4

100 g (4 oz) butter
100 g (4 oz) caster sugar
2 large eggs, beaten
grated rind of 1 small orange
100 g (4 oz) self-raising flour
pinch of salt
1 tbls fresh orange juice
2 tbls golden syrup
142 ml (5 fl oz) carton single cream, to finish

In a large bowl, cream the butter and sugar together until light and fluffy. Beat in the eggs a little at a time, with the orange rind. Sift the flour with the salt and fold into the creamed mixture, then add the orange juice.

Grease a 900 ml (1½ pint) foil pudding basin, place the golden syrup in the bottom and spoon in the sponge mixture. Cover with buttered heavy duty foil with a pleat in the centre to allow for expansion. Secure the foil around the rim of the basin with string. Stand the basin in a saucepan with boiling water one third of the way up the sides of the basin and steam for 1½-2 hours, until cooked through.

To freeze: Cool quickly, wrap in cling film and overwrap in foil or polythene bag. Seal, label and freeze for up to 3 months.
To serve: Thaw at room temperature for 4 hours. Reheat by steaming for 45 minutes, as above. Serve with cream.
Variations: Use 2 tbls marmalade along with, or instead of, the grated orange rind. This pudding can also be made with other flavourings: replace the orange with 1 lemon or 2 limes. Use 25 g (1 oz) chopped stem ginger, and 2 tbls of the ginger syrup instead of the golden syrup. Use 1 tsp ground ginger, and 2 tbls treacle instead of syrup.

• Blackberry and apple whip; Orange syrup pudding

Grapefruit sorbet

SERVES 6

100 g (4 oz) caster sugar
250 ml (8 fl oz) water
175 ml (6¼ fl oz) can frozen concentrated grapefruit juice
grated rind and juice of 1 grapefruit
2 egg whites
To decorate
grapefruit segments
mint sprigs

Place the sugar and water in a small saucepan. Stir over low heat for 3-4 minutes, until the sugar has dissolved. Increase the heat and boil for 1 minute without stirring, then remove from the heat and allow to cool. Add the concentrated juice and the rind and juice of the grapefruit.

Pour into a shallow rigid container and place in the freezer for 1 hour or until mushy. Turn the mixture into a large bowl and beat until smooth. In another bowl, whisk the egg whites stiffly, then fold into the sorbet. Return to the container.

To freeze: Cover, seal, label and freeze for up to 3 months.
To serve: The sorbet is served frozen, but should be placed in the refrigerator for 15 minutes before serving, to soften slightly. Scoop into individual glass bowls and decorate with grapefruit segments and mint sprigs to serve.
Variation: For orange sorbet, use frozen concentrated orange juice and rind and juice of 2 oranges. For an impressive party dessert for 12, set the grapefruit sorbet in a ring mould and make the orange sorbet in an ice tray. To serve, turn out the grapefruit ring and fill the centre with scoops of orange sorbet. For apricot sorbet use 450 ml (¾ pint) apricot puree with 2 tbls lemon juice and 3 drops almond essence.

Sparkling wine ice cream

SERVES 4-6

350 g (12 oz) caster sugar
300 ml (½ pint) water
2 tbls orange juice
1 tbls brandy
450 ml (¾ pint) sparkling white wine
142 ml (5 fl oz) carton double or whipping cream
shredded orange rind, to decorate

Place the sugar and water in a small heavy-based saucepan. Stir over low heat for 3-4 minutes, until the sugar has dissolved. Increase the heat and boil, without stirring, until the syrup registers 107°C, 225°F on a sugar thermometer, or test by removing a little of the syrup with a small spoon and allowing it to fall from the spoon on to a dish. The syrup should form a fine thin thread. Remove from the heat and allow to cool.

In a small bowl, combine the orange juice, brandy and wine and stir into the syrup. Pour the mixture into a shallow rigid container. Place in the freezer for 1 hour or until mushy.

Whip the cream in a bowl until soft peaks form. Turn the frozen wine mixture into a bowl and fold in the cream. Return to the freezer. After 1 hour turn the ice cream out again into a bowl and beat well, preferably with a hand-held electric beater. Return the ice cream to the freezer. Repeat this twice more at hourly intervals.

To freeze: Cover, seal, label and freeze for up to 3 months.
To serve: Thaw at room temperature for 10 minutes before serving in scoops, sprinkled with orange rind. Serve, if liked, with crisp sugar biscuits.
Variation: Cointreau or Grand Marnier may be used instead of brandy.

• Top: Sparkling wine ice cream; Left: Honey and brandy mousse
Right: Grapefruit sorbet

Honey and brandy mousse

SERVES 6

3 eggs, separated
2 tbls clear honey
2 tbls lemon juice
2 tbls brandy
2 tbls water
142 ml (5 fl oz) double cream, lightly whipped
toasted chopped nuts, to decorate
fan wafers, to serve

In a large bowl, beat the egg yolks with the honey, lemon juice, brandy and water until the mixture is thick and light and has doubled in volume. In another bowl, beat the egg whites stiffly, then fold into the egg yolk mixture. Fold in the cream. Spoon into 6 ramekins.

To freeze: Open freeze until solid, then wrap in cling film and overwrap in foil or place in polythene bags. Seal, label and freeze for up to 2 months.
To serve: Serve frozen, but place in the refrigerator for 30 minutes before serving, to soften slightly. Sprinkle with nuts and serve with wafers.
Variation: Whisky may be used in place of the brandy.

Apple strudel

SERVES 6-8

For the dough
1 egg
150 ml (¼ pint) water
300 g (11 oz) plain flour, sifted
For the filling
1 kg (2 lb) cooking apples, peeled, cored and finely chopped
40 g (1½ oz) crushed cornflakes
4 tbls clear honey
½ tsp ground cinnamon
50 g (2 oz) walnuts, chopped
100 g (4 oz) butter, melted
To serve
sifted icing sugar
142 ml (5 fl oz) carton whipping cream

Heat the oven to 190°C, 375°F, Gas Mark 5.

In a large bowl, beat the egg and water together with a wooden spoon. Add the flour and mix to a slightly sticky dough.

Turn the dough on to a lightly floured board. Slap the dough on to the board repeatedly with flicking wrist movements for about 5 minutes, to make it smooth and elastic. Then knead it lightly for a further 3 minutes.

Place the dough in a lightly floured bowl, cover with cling film and leave to rest for 10 minutes.

Meanwhile, mix the apples, cornflakes, honey, cinnamon and nuts in a second bowl with 1 tbls of the butter. Divide the dough in half and wrap one half in cling film. Roll out the remaining dough to a 50 × 30 cm (20 × 12 inch) rectangle, stretching the dough gently with floured hands.

Cut the rectangle in half lengthways. Brush each strip with melted butter

and spread evenly with half the filling. Fold a 1 cm (½ inch) margin down each long side, then roll up from a long edge. Repeat with the remaining dough.

Place the strudel on a lightly greased baking sheet, brush all over with melted butter and bake for 25-30 minutes or until lightly coloured.

To freeze: Cool quickly. Open freeze until solid, then wrap in cling film and place in a polythene bag. Seal, label and freeze for up to 6 months.
To serve: Thaw in wrappings for 2 hours at room temperature. Serve cold or to serve hot, unwrap, place on a baking sheet and reheat in a 190°C, 375°F, Gas Mark 5 oven for 20 minutes. Slice, dredge with icing sugar and serve with whipped cream.
Variation: 4 tbls currants may be added to the filling, if liked.

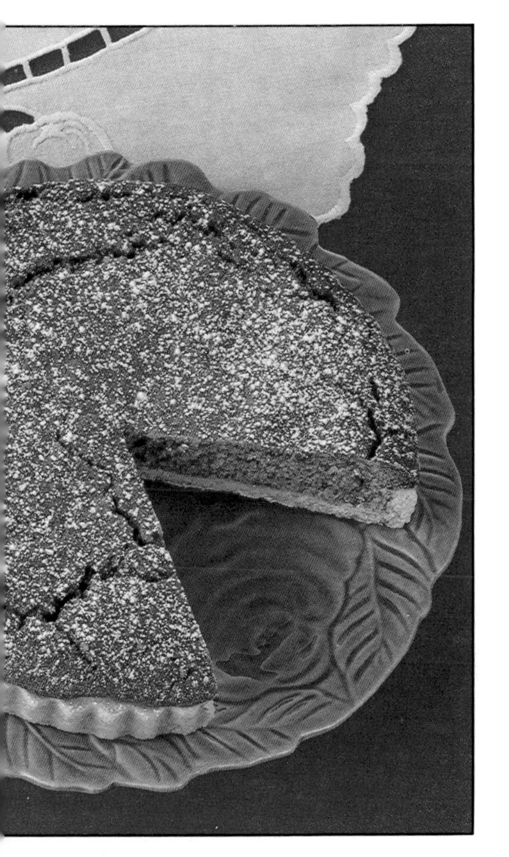

Walnut flan

SERVES 6

For the pastry
225 g (8 oz) plain flour
½ tsp salt
50 g (2 oz) butter, diced
50 g (2 oz) margarine, diced
1-2 tbls cold water
For the filling
100 g (4 oz) butter
100 g (4 oz) brown sugar
1 large egg, beaten
50 g (2 oz) walnuts, finely chopped
100 g (4 oz) self-raising flour, sifted with ½ teaspoon cinnamon
1 tbls milk

Heat the oven to 220°C, 425°F, Gas Mark 7.

Sift the flour with the salt into a mixing bowl. Add the fats and rub in with the fingertips until the mixture resembles fine breadcrumbs. Stir in enough cold water to mix to a firm dough. Turn on to a floured surface and knead lightly for 1 minute. Wrap in foil and chill in the refrigerator for 30 minutes. Roll out on a floured board and use to line a 20 cm (8 inch) flan ring on a baking sheet.

To make the filling, cream the butter and sugar together in a bowl until fluffy. Beat in the egg and walnuts and fold in the sifted flour and cinnamon alternately with the milk. Spoon the mixture into the flan case. Smooth the top with a knife and bake in the oven for 15 minutes, then reduce the temperature to 160°C, 325°F, Gas Mark 3, and bake for 25 minutes or until browned.

To freeze: Cool quickly, place in a polythene bag, seal, label and freeze for up to 2 months.
To serve: Remove the flan from the bag and thaw in the refrigerator overnight. Reheat in a 160°C, 325°F, Gas Mark 3 oven for 20 minutes.

• Apple strudel
Walnut flan

Coffee cake

100g (4oz) margarine or butter, softened
100g (4oz) caster sugar
1 tbls instant coffee powder dissolved in 1 tbls boiling water
75g (3oz) plain flour
1 tsp baking powder
pinch of salt
2 eggs, well beaten
50g (2oz) ground almonds
For the icing
50g (2oz) butter, softened
100g (4oz) icing sugar, sifted
1 tbls instant coffee powder, dissolved in 1 tbls boiling water
8 walnut halves, to finish

Heat the oven to 190°C, 375°F, Gas Mark 5.

In a large bowl, cream the margarine with the sugar until light and fluffy, then beat in the dissolved coffee. Sift the flour with the baking powder and salt into another bowl, then fold 2 tbls into the creamed mixture. Beat in the eggs, a little at a time, then fold in the remaining flour and the ground almonds with a large metal spoon.

Butter two 18cm (7 inch) sandwich tins and divide the mixture evenly between them. Bake in the oven for 20-25 minutes, until the cakes are risen and shrunk from the sides of the tins. Remove the cakes from the oven and allow to cool for 10 minutes in the tins, then turn them out on to a wire rack and leave to cool completely.

To make the icing, cream the butter and icing sugar together in a bowl, then beat in the dissolved coffee. Use half the icing to sandwich the cakes together and spread the remainder over the top. Swirl the icing decoratively into a wave pattern with a fork and decorate with the walnut halves.

To freeze: Open freeze until solid, then wrap in cling film and overwrap in foil or place in a rigid container. Seal, label and freeze for up to 3 months.
To serve: Unwrap, transfer to a plate and thaw for 2½-3 hours at room temperature.

Lemon dairy sponge

3 eggs
75g (3oz) caster sugar
75g (3oz) self-raising flour, sifted
For the filling
142ml (5fl oz) carton double cream
2 tbls lemon curd
2 tbls icing sugar, to decorate

Heat the oven to 190°C, 375°F, Gas Mark 5.

Grease two 18cm (7 inch) sandwich tins and line them with greased greaseproof paper. Place the eggs and sugar in a heatproof bowl set over a saucepan of hot water and whisk until the mixture is thick and pale and the whisk leaves a trail when lifted. Remove from the heat and whisk for a further 2 minutes. Lightly fold in the flour.

Divide the mixture equally between the tins and bake in the oven for 20 minutes, or until the cakes are risen and the tops spring back when lightly pressed with the fingertips. Turn on to a wire rack and leave to cool completely.

In a bowl, whip the cream until thick and blend in the lemon curd. Use to sandwich the cakes together.

To freeze: Open freeze until solid, then wrap in cling film and overwrap in foil. Seal, label and freeze up to 3 months.
To serve: Thaw in wrappings for 4 hours at room temperature. Unwrap, place on a dish and sift with the icing sugar.

• Top: Lemon dairy sponge; Bottom: Coffee cake

Devil's food cake

75g (3oz) plain chocolate, broken into pieces
175ml (6fl oz) strong black coffee
175g (6oz) unsalted butter
225g (8oz) soft dark brown sugar
50g (2oz) caster sugar
3 eggs
a few drops vanilla essence
275g (10oz) plain flour
1½tsp bicarbonate of soda
175ml (6fl oz) soured cream
For the icing
450g (1 lb) sugar
300ml (½pint) water
2 egg whites

Heat the oven to 190°C, 375°F, Gas Mark 5.

Place the chocolate in a saucepan with the coffee and stir over low heat until the chocolate has melted and the mixture is smooth. Set aside to cool.

Grease three 20cm (8 inch) sandwich tins and line with greased greaseproof paper. Dust the paper with flour and tap off the excess.

In a large bowl, beat the butter until pale and creamy. Add the sugars and beat until fluffy. Add the eggs, one at a time, beating well after each addition. Stir in the vanilla essence and melted chocolate. Sift the flour with the bicarbonate of soda on to a sheet of greaseproof paper and fold into the chocolate mixture in 2 or 3 additions, alternating with the soured cream.

Divide the mixture equally among the tins and bake in the oven for 25 minutes or until the cakes have shrunk from the sides of the tins. Remove from the oven and allow to cool for 10 minutes in the tins, then turn on to a wire rack and leave to cool completely.

To make the icing, place the sugar and water in a small heavy-based saucepan. Stir over low heat until the sugar has dissolved. Increase the heat and boil, without stirring, until the syrup registers 115°C, 238°F on a sugar thermometer, or test by dropping a small amount of the syrup into iced water. Mould the sticky syrup into a soft ball with the fingers. Remove the ball from the water – it should immediately lose its shape.

When this stage is reached, remove the pan from the heat and lower the base carefully into warm water to prevent further cooking. Whisk the egg whites stiffly in a large bowl. Gradually whisk the sugar syrup into the whisked egg whites. Continue whisking until the icing thickens and loses its sheen. Immediately use to sandwich together the cake layers and swirl over the top and sides of the cake.

To freeze: Open freeze until solid, then wrap in cling film and overwrap in foil or place in a polythene bag or rigid container. Seal, label and freeze for up to 3 months.
To serve: Unwrap, transfer to a cake plate or dish and thaw overnight in the refrigerator, or for 2½-3 hours at room temperature.

• Devil's food cake; Apple, nut and sultana loaf

Apple, nut and sultana loaf

165 g (5½ oz) margarine or butter
225 g (8 oz) sugar
2 eggs, beaten
225 g (8 oz) plain flour
1 tsp bicarbonate of soda
1 tsp mixed spice
75 g (3 oz) sultanas
50 g (2 oz) walnuts, finely chopped
225 g (8 oz) apple purée
sifted icing sugar, to finish

Heat the oven to 180°C, 350°F, Gas Mark 4.

Grease a 10 × 25 cm (4 × 10 inch) loaf tin and line with greased greaseproof paper.

In a large bowl, cream the margarine with the sugar until light and fluffy. Add the eggs, a little at a time. Sift the flour with the soda and spice on to a sheet of greaseproof paper, then fold into the creamed mixture. Stir in the sultanas, walnuts and apple purée.

Spoon the mixture into the prepared tin, smooth the top and bake in the oven for 1 hour, or until a fine skewer inserted in the loaf comes out clean. Remove from the oven and leave to cool in the tin for 10 minutes, then turn on to a wire rack and leave to cool.

To freeze: Wrap in cling film, overwrap in foil or place in a polythene bag, seal, label and freeze for up to 4 months.
To serve: Thaw in wrappings at room temperature for 4 hours, then unwrap and place on a cake platter. Dust with icing sugar.

Freezer cookies

MAKES ABOUT 40

225 g (8 oz) plain flour
1 tsp baking powder
100 g (4 oz) butter, diced
175 g (6 oz) caster sugar
1 tsp vanilla essence
1 egg, beaten

Sift the flour with the baking powder into a large bowl. Add the butter and rub in with the fingertips until the mixture resembles fine breadcrumbs. Stir in the sugar, vanilla essence and beaten egg and mix to a smooth dough.

Turn the dough on to a floured surface and knead for 2 minutes. Wrap in foil, then chill in the refrigerator for about 15 minutes.

Shape the dough into a long roll, about 5 cm (2 inches) in diameter.

To freeze: Wrap the dough in cling film, overwrap in foil, seal, label and freeze for up to 6 months.
To serve: Unwrap the dough and thaw for 1 hour in the refrigerator. Cut into slices 1 cm (½ inch) thick and place on a greased baking sheet. Bake in a 190°c. 375°F, Gas Mark 5 oven for 10 minutes, or until the biscuits are light golden. Remove from the oven and leave to firm for 2 minutes on the baking sheet, then transfer to a wire rack and leave to cool completely.

Chocolate fork biscuits

MAKES ABOUT 36

225 g (8 oz) butter
100 g (4 oz) caster sugar
1 tsp vanilla essence
225 g (8 oz) self-raising flour
50 g (2 oz) drinking chocolate powder

In a large bowl, cream the butter with the sugar until light and fluffy. Stir in the vanilla essence and fold in the flour and chocolate powder.

Divide the mixture into walnut-sized pieces and roll into balls. Place on a baking sheet and flatten with a large fork dipped in cold water.

To freeze: Open freeze until solid, pack into a rigid container, cover, label and freeze for up to 6 months.
To serve: Remove the biscuits from the freezer and place on a greased baking sheet, at least 5 cm (2 inches) apart. Bake from frozen in a 190°C, 375°F, Gas Mark 5 oven for 12-15 minutes. Leave the biscuits to firm for 1 minute on the baking sheet, then transfer them to a wire rack to cool.
Variations: To make lemon or orange fork biscuits add 2 tsp grated lemon or orange rind instead of the chocolate. For a ginger flavour use 1 tsp ground ginger.

Fruit scones

MAKES 12-14

225 g (8 oz) plain flour
pinch of salt
1 tsp mixed spice
½ tsp cream of tartar
½ tsp bicarbonate of soda
40 g (1½ oz) chilled butter, diced
25 g (1 oz) caster sugar
25 g (1 oz) sultanas
15 g (½ oz) currants
15 g (½ oz) cut mixed peel
about 150 ml (¼ pint) milk
a little milk, to glaze

Heat the oven to 230°C, 450°F, Gas Mark 8.

Sift the flour with the salt, mixed spice, cream of tartar and bicarbonate of soda into a mixing bowl. Add the butter and rub in with the fingertips until the mixture resembles fine breadcrumbs. Stir in the sugar, sultanas, currants and mixed peel.

Stir in enough milk to make a soft dough. Turn on to a floured surface, knead very lightly for 1 minute, then roll or pat out to 1 cm (½ inch) thick. Cut into 12-14 rounds with a 5 cm (2 inch) biscuit cutter.

Place the scones on a floured baking sheet and brush the tops with a little milk.

Bake in the oven for 10-12 minutes, until well risen and golden brown. Transfer the scones to a wire rack and leave to cool completely.

To freeze: Place the scones in a polythene bag, seal, label and freeze for up to 6 months.
To serve: Remove the scones from the freezer and place on a baking sheet. Reheat from frozen in a 180°C, 350°F, Gas Mark 4 oven for about 10 minutes. Serve split and buttered.

• **From left to right: Freezer cookies; Chocolate fork biscuits; Fruit scones**

SUMMER DINNER PARTY

Avocado Ice Cream

Sole Véronique

Caramel Oranges

•

Muscadet

Touraine Sauvignon

Avocado ice cream

SERVES 4

2 large ripe avocado pears
75 g (3 oz) full fat soft cheese
1 shallot, finely chopped
1 tbls lemon juice
2 tbls natural yoghurt
1 tsp sugar
dash of Worcestershire sauce
pinch of freshly grated nutmeg
pinch of paprika
salt and pepper
To garnish
4 tbls mayonnaise
100 g (4 oz) peeled prawns
lemon twists
parsley sprigs

Peel and halve the avocado pears and remove the stones. Chop the flesh and place in an electric blender or food processor with the remaining ingredients and process until thoroughly blended.

Spoon the mixture into a 600 ml (1 pint) rigid container and freeze for at least 1½-2 hours, beating thoroughly 2 or 3 times to prevent any crystals from forming.

To freeze: When fully frozen, cover the ice cream, label and freeze for up to 3 months.

To serve: Thaw in the refrigerator for 1 hour before serving. To serve, turn out on to a serving dish and garnish with swirls of mayonnaise, prawns, lemon twists and parsley.

• Avocado ice cream
Sole Véronique

Sole Véronique

SERVES 4

4 large sole fillets, skinned
1 1/2 tbls lemon juice
1 small onion, chopped
1 parsley sprig
6 whole black peppercorns
salt and white pepper
175 ml (6 fl oz) dry white wine
300 ml (1/2 pint) Béchamel sauce (see page 61)
175 g (6 oz) green grapes, skinned, halved and seeded

Heat the oven to 190°C, 375°F, Gas Mark 5.

Fold each sole fillet into three and arrange in a buttered ovenproof dish. Sprinkle over the lemon juice and add the onion, parsley, peppercorns and salt and pepper. Pour in the white wine with enough water barely to cover the sole. Cover with foil and bake in the oven for 20 minutes.

Lift out the sole and set aside. Pour the cooking liquid into a saucepan and boil briskly for 5 minutes, then strain and reserve 50 ml (2 fl oz). Place the sole in a buttered shallow foil container. Stir the reduced cooling liquid and the milk into the béchamel sauce. Bring to the boil, stirring constantly, until the sauce thickens. Adjust the seasoning to taste, fold in the grapes and pour the sauce over the fish fillets.

To freeze: Cool quickly, cover, seal, label and freeze for up to 1 month.
To serve: Remove the cover and thaw at room temperature for 4 hours. Transfer to an ovenproof serving dish, cover and reheat in a 180°C, 350°F, Gas Mark 4 oven for 40-50 minutes or until heated through.

• Caramel oranges

Caramel oranges

SERVES 4

100g (4oz) caster sugar
250ml (8fl oz) water
4 large oranges, peeled and all pith removed
1-2 tbls Curaçao or other orange-flavoured liqueur, to serve
shredded orange zest, to decorate

Place the sugar and half the water in a small heavy-based saucepan. Stir over low heat for 3-4 minutes, until the sugar has dissolved. Increase the heat and boil, without stirring, until the syrup registers 168°C, 336°F on a sugar thermometer, or test by removing a little of the syrup with a small spoon and pouring it on to a white saucer. The syrup should be a light golden brown colour. Do not allow it to become too dark or the flavour will be spoilt and become bitter. As soon as the syrup caramelizes, lower the base of the pan carefully into warm water to arrest further cooking.

Allow the caramel mixture to cool, then add the remaining water and return the saucepan to a low heat. Stir constantly until the caramel mixture become smooth, then remove from the heat and set aside.

Using a sharp knife, carefully segment the oranges, cutting cleanly between the segments and removing any pith adhering to them. Do this over the saucepan so that any juice drips into the caramel syrup.

Place the orange segments in a shallow rigid container, and strain the caramel syrup over them.

To freeze: Seal, label and freeze for up to 1 year.

To serve: Thaw overnight in the refrigerator or for 4 hours at room temperature. Transfer the oranges and syrup to a glass bowl, stir in the Curaçao and serve chilled decorated with orange zest and accompanied by brandy snaps filled with whipped cream or scoops of vanilla ice cream.

WINTER DINNER PARTY

Camembert Crescents

Normandy Pork

Chestnut Vacherin

•

Anjou Rosé

Premières Côtes de Bordeaux

Camembert crescents

SERVES 6

225g (8oz) Camembert cheese, rinded
1 tbls snipped fresh chives
pinch of freshly grated nutmeg
pepper
1 tbls double cream
370g (13oz) packet frozen puff pastry, thawed
1 egg, beaten, to serve
spring onion tassels, to garnish

Place the Camembert cheese in a bowl, mash well with a fork until smooth and stir in the chives, nutmeg, pepper and cream.

Roll out the pastry on a floured board, and cut into 12 squares, each 15cm (6inches). Cut each square in half diagonally.

Place 1 tsp of the Camembert mixture along the longest edge of each of the triangles, then roll them up to enclose the filling.

Twist the ends and curve them round to form a crescent shape. Place the crescents on a baking sheet.

To freeze: Open freeze until solid, then pack the crescents in a rigid container, cover, seal, label and freeze for up to 4 months.

To serve: Place the crescents on a baking sheet and brush lightly with the beaten egg. Bake in a 200°C, 400°F, Gas Mark 7 oven for 20 minutes, until risen and lightly browned. Serve garnished with spring onion tassels.

• Camembert crescents

Normandy pork

SERVES 6

100g (4oz) pork fat, diced
1 large onion, finely chopped
1 kg (2 lb) pork fillet, cut into strips
450g (1 lb) tart dessert apples
2 tbls Calvados or 4 tbls cider
284 ml (10fl oz) carton double cream
salt and pepper
1 tbls chopped fresh parsley

Fry the pork fat in a large flameproof casserole until crisp. Pour off all but 2 tbls of the fat, add the onion and cook gently for 1-2 minutes.

Add the pork, increase the heat and fry briskly, turning, to seal and brown on all sides.

Peel, core and finely chop the apples. Add to the casserole, cover and cook over very low heat for 20-30 minutes, until the pork is tender and the apples are cooked to a thick purée.

Increase the heat, add the Calvados or cider and allow to bubble for 1 minute. Pour in the cream and cook gently until the sauce thickens, stirring constantly. Remove from the heat and season to taste with salt and pepper.

To freeze: Cool quickly, transfer to a foil or rigid polythene container, cover, label and freeze for up to 6 weeks.
To serve: Turn the casserole into a large saucepan, add 2 tbls water or cider, and reheat gently from frozen for about 45 minutes, stirring and turning the block occasionally. Adjust the seasoning to taste, garnish with chopped parsley and serve with croquette potatoes and red cabbage. Or serve with creamy mashed potato into which is beaten 1 egg for every 450g (1lb) of potatoes, lightly flavoured with nutmeg and baked at 180°C, 350°F, Gas Mark 4 for 30 minutes. Instead of the red cabbage serve green cabbage, quartered, steamed, buttered and well seasoned.

Chestnut vacherin

SERVES 6

For the meringue
6 egg whites
350g (12oz) caster sugar
For the filling
284 ml (10fl oz) carton double cream
1 tbls milk
250g (8¾oz) can sweetened chestnut purée
grated chocolate, to decorate

Heat the oven to its lowest setting.

Line 3 baking sheets with greased greaseproof paper, and mark a 23 cm (9 inch) circle on each.

Place the egg whites in a clean dry bowl and whisk stiffly. Whisk in half the sugar, whisk again for 1 minute, then, using a metal spoon, fold in the remaining sugar. Spoon equal amounts of meringue on to each baking sheet and spread evenly over each circle, using a palette knife.

Bake the meringue layers in the oven for about 4 hours or until crisp. Remove from the oven and leave to cool completely on the trays, then carefully peel off the greaseproof paper.

To make the filling, whisk the cream with the milk until soft peaks form. Fold in the chestnut purée and use to sandwich together the meringue layers.

To freeze: Open freeze until solid, then place in a rigid container. Seal, label and freeze for up to 6 months.
To serve: Unwrap, transfer to a serving dish and thaw for 3 hours at room temperature. Decorate the top with grated chocolate.

Variations: If liked, 50g (2oz) melted and cooled plain dessert chocolate may be stirred into the chestnut purée. The chestnut purée may also be flavoured with 2 tbls strong black coffee, or the finely grated rind of 1 small orange.

• Normandy pork; Chestnut vacherin

Christmas is the season of good cheer, and for many cooks that cheer is simply "Thank goodness that's over".

Yet Christmas dinner needn't be much more difficult to prepare than the average Sunday lunch, provided you plan the meal carefully.

Your freezer is your best friend here, and our easy recipes make it possible for you to do most of the cooking long before you get your first Christmas card.

CHRISTMAS DINNER

Smoked Salmon Pâté

Turkey with Chestnut Stuffing, Apricot Nut Stuffing and Cranberry Sauce

Mince Pies

•

Bourgogne Rouge

Sauternes

Smoked salmon pâté

SERVES 6

1 large avocado pear
225 g (8 oz) full fat soft cheese
3 tbls lemon juice
175 g (6 oz) smoked salmon
salt and pepper
pinch of cayenne
pinch of grated nutmeg
2 tbls double cream
2 tbls finely chopped watercress
To garnish
rolls of smoked salmon
4 watercress sprigs
lemon wedges

Peel and halve the avocado pear and remove the stone. Chop the flesh and place in a blender or food processor together with the cheese, lemon juice and 100 g (4 oz) of the smoked salmon. Process until smooth. Season with salt, pepper, cayenne and nutmeg.

Chop the remaining smoked salmon finely and stir it into the mixture with the cream and chopped watercress.

To freeze: Spoon the mixture into a rigid container, cover, label and freeze for up to 6 weeks.
To serve: Thaw in the refrigerator overnight. Spoon the pâté into individual ramekins, garnish each portion with a roll of smoked salmon, a watercress sprig and lemon wedge.

Stuffed roast turkey with cranberry sauce

SERVES 16-20

A turkey is only worth freezing if you have a large freezer with plenty of space to spare.

Whether you freeze a turkey yourself or buy it ready-frozen just before Christmas, *it is vital* to thaw it thoroughly before cooking. A 4.5-5.5 kg (10-12 lb) turkey will require at least 36 hours thawing time in a refrigerator, or 12 hours at room temperature, but if the latter procedure is followed, the bird must be cooked as soon as it is completely thawed. Ready-frozen turkeys usually have thawing times clearly listed on the packaging.

Do not stuff a bird before freezing. Prepare the stuffings up to 3 months before Christmas, freeze them in rigid containers and thaw before using.

The Cranberry sauce is also made in advance and frozen until required.

4.5-5.5 kg (10-12 lb) turkey, thawed
Chestnut Stuffing (below)
Apricot Nut Stuffing (below)
225 g (8 oz) streaky bacon rashers
chipolata sausages and bacon rolls (optional)

• **Smoked salmon pâté; Stuffed roast turkey with cranberry sauce**

Heat the oven to 190°C, 375°F, Gas Mark 5.

Remove the giblets and wash and dry the turkey thoroughly. Loosely pack the Chestnut stuffing into the neck end, drawing back the neck skin to enclose it. Turn the turkey breast side up and tuck the wings under the body to hold the neck skin in place.

Spoon the Apricot nut stuffing into the body cavity. Truss the bird and weigh it, calculating the cooking time at 15 minutes per 450 g (1 lb), plus 15 minutes. Place the turkey breast side up in a roasting tin. Cover the breast with bacon rashers.

Cover the turkey with foil and roast in the oven for the calculated time, basting frequently. Remove the foil for the last 1 hour of cooking. Add the chipolatas 45 minutes and the bacon rolls 30 minutes before the end of cooking. Remove the bacon slices from the turkey breast when the bacon rolls are added, to allow the breast to brown.

Serve the turkey surrounded by the chipolatas and bacon rolls, and accompanied by roast potatoes, carrots cooked in orange juice, and brussels sprouts with chestnuts. Hand the Cranberry sauce separately.

Chestnut stuffing

SUFFICIENT TO STUFF A 4.5-5.5 kg (10-12 lb) TURKEY

450 g (1 lb) fresh chestnuts
300 ml (½ pint) Beef stock (see page 60)
100 g (4 oz) fresh wholemeal breadcrumbs
finely grated rind of ½ lemon
salt and pepper
50 g (2 oz) butter
1 small onion, finely chopped
a little milk

Make a slit in each chestnut with a sharp knife. Place the chestnuts in a saucepan, add water to cover, bring to the boil and boil for 5 minutes. Remove from the heat, drain and peel the chestnuts when cool enough to handle. Return the chestnuts to the rinsed out pan, add the stock and simmer for 20-30 minutes, or until tender.

Drain the chestnuts and sieve or purée in a food mill or blender.

Place the chestnut purée, breadcrumbs and lemon rind in a bowl. Season to taste with salt and pepper and stir well to mix.

Melt the butter in a small saucepan, add the onion and fry gently for 5 minutes until soft and lightly coloured Stir the onion into the breadcrumb mixture and mix well, adding enough milk just to bind.

To freeze: Pack into a rigid container, seal, label and freeze for up to 3 months.
To serve: Thaw at room temperature for 3 hours. Use as directed in the Roast turkey recipe.

Cranberry sauce

MAKES ABOUT 450 ml (¾ pint)

300 ml (½ pint) water
2 tsp lemon juice
100 g (4 oz) sugar
225 g (8 oz) fresh or frozen cranberries
25 g (1 oz) butter, softened

Place the water, lemon juice and sugar in a small heavy-based saucepan. Stir over low heat for 3-4 minutes, until the sugar has dissolved.

Add the cranberries, increase the heat and cook briskly for 2-3 minutes, until the skins pop. Reduce the heat and simmer uncovered, stirring occasionally, for 15-20 minutes, or until soft and pulpy. Remove from the heat and beat in the butter.

If a smoother sauce is preferred, rub the mixture through a sieve.

To freeze: Cool quickly, transfer to a small rigid container, seal, label and freeze for up to 1 year.
To serve: Thaw at room temperature for 3-4 hours or reheat in a small saucepan over low heat for 10-15 minutes or until heated through.

Apricot nut stuffing

MAKES ABOUT 450 g (1 lb)

100 g (4 oz) dried apricots, soaked in cold water to cover for 1 hour, drained and chopped
100 g (4 oz) fresh white breadcrumbs
50 g (2 oz) hazelnuts, finely chopped
1 tbls chopped fresh parsley
50 g (2 oz) butter
1 small onion, finely chopped
finely grated rind and juice of 1 orange
1 egg, beaten
salt and pepper

Place the apricots in a bowl, add the breadcrumbs, hazelnuts and parsley and stir well to mix.

Melt the butter in a saucepan, add the onion and fry gently for 5 minutes until soft and lightly coloured. Stir in the apricot and breadcrumb mixture. Add the orange rind, juice and egg and seaon to taste with salt and pepper. Stir well to mix.

To freeze: Pack into a rigid container, seal, label and freeze for up to 3 months.
To serve: Thaw at room temperature for 4 hours.

• Stuffed roast turkey; Centre: Chestnut stuffing; Bottom: Apricot nut stuffing

Iced Christmas pudding

SERVES 6

Delicious though the traditional Christmas pudding may be, it is certainly not light! After a hearty turkey dinner, why not try our iced Christmas pudding? It's tasty, festive, and, with liberal use of fruits and brandy, full of the Christmas spirit.

1 tbls glacé cherries, roughly chopped
1 tbls sultanas, roughly chopped
2 tbls glacé pineapple, roughly chopped
1 tbls currants
2 tbls brandy or Kirsch
600 ml (1 pint) vanilla ice cream, softened
To serve
142 ml (5 fl oz) carton whipping cream
glacé cherries
angelica

Place the fruit in a large bowl, add the brandy and leave to macerate for 2 hours.

Place the ice cream in a bowl and beat until smooth. Stir in the macerated fruits and liquor and mix well. Spoon the mixture into a 900 ml (1 ½ pint) foil basin.

To freeze: Wrap in cling film, overwrap in a polythene bag, seal, label and freeze for up to 3 months.
To serve: Unwrap, unmould, place on a serving dish and soften at room temperature for 15 minutes. Pipe the cream round the base of the pudding and decorate with small pieces of glacé cherries and angelica. This pudding may also be decorated with blanched almonds and mixed glacé fruits.

Mince pies

MAKES 12

225 g (8 oz) plain flour
¼ tsp salt
150 g (5 oz) butter, diced
15 g (½ oz) caster sugar
15 g (½ oz) ground almonds
1-2 tbls cold water
350 g (12 oz) mincemeat
To glaze
1 egg, beaten
a little caster sugar

Sift the flour with the salt into a mixing bowl. Add the butter and rub in with the fingertips until the mixture resembles fine breadcrumbs. Stir in the sugar and almonds. Using a knife, mix in enough water to make a stiff crumbly dough. Draw the dough together with the fingertips, and turn on to a floured board. Knead lightly for 1 minute, then wrap in foil and chill in the refrigerator for 30 minutes.

Roll out the pastry thinly and cut out 24 circles: use a 7.5 cm (3 inch) cutter to cut out 12 circles, and a 6.5 cm (2½ inch) cutter to cut out the remainder. Use the larger circles to line 12 deep patty tins. Divide the mincemeat equally between them. Dampen the edges of the pastry and cover with the smaller circles, sealing the edges well.

To freeze: Open freeze in the tins until solid. Then remove the pies from the tins, pack carefully in a rigid container, seal, label and freeze for up to 3 months.
To serve: Return the frozen mince pies to the patty tins, brush them with beaten egg, sprinkle with a little caster sugar and bake in a 200°C, 400°F, Gas Mark 6 oven for 20 minutes or until golden brown.

• **Iced Christmas pudding; Mince pies**

Basic beef stock

MAKES 1¾-2¼ litres (3-4 pints)

1.5 kg (3 lb) shin or neck of beef bones
2 large carrots, sliced
2 large onions, sliced
1 leek, sliced
1 celery stalk, sliced
1 bay leaf
1 sprig fresh thyme
1 sprig fresh parsley
1 tsp salt
6 whole black peppercorns
2 cloves

Chop the beef bones into pieces and place in a large saucepan. Cover with cold water and add the remaining ingredients.

Bring slowly to the boil, skimming off the scum that rises to the surface with a slotted spoon. Cover, reduce the heat and simmer gently for at least 2-3 hours, adding more water if the level drops below that of the bones.

Remove from the heat, strain and cool. Remove any surface fat.

To freeze: Cool quickly, then pour the stock, in small quantities if desired, into rigid containers. Cover, seal, label and freeze for up to 3 months. Or boil the strained stock unti reduced by one half, cool quickly and freeze in ice cube trays. Transfer the frozen stock cubes to a polythene bag, seal, label and freeze for up to 3 months.

To serve: Turn the frozen stock into a saucepan, add 2 tbls water and reheat gently for about 30 minutes, stirring and turning the block occasionally. Or add the frozen cubes to soups or casseroles.

Variation: For chicken stock, replace the beef bones with 2 chicken carcases.

Fish stock

MAKES 900 ml-1 litre (1½-1¾ pints)

450 g (1 lb) white fish trimmings (head, bones, tails)
1.2 litres (2 pints) cold water
1 onion, roughly chopped
1 celery stalk, sliced
1 bouquet garni
1 strip thinly pared lemon rind
¼ tsp salt
6 whole green peppercorns

Place the fish trimmings in a colander and rinse under cold running water. Transfer to a large saucepan. Cover with the cold water, bring slowly to the boil and skim off the scum that rises to the surface with a slotted spoon.

Add the remaining ingredients, return to the boil, cover, reduce the heat and simmer for 20 minutes, skimming when necessary.

Remove from the heat and strain.

To freeze: Cool quickly, then pour the stock, in small quantities if desired, into rigid containers. Cover, seal, label and freeze for up to 3 months. Or boil the strained stock until reduced by half, cool quickly and freeze in ice cube trays. Transfer the frozen stock cubes to a polythene bag, seal, label and freeze for up to 3 months.

To serve: Turn the frozen stock into a saucepan, add 2 tbls water and reheat gently for about 30 minutes, stirring and turning the block occasionally. Or add the frozen cubes to soups or casseroles.

• Left: Fish stock; Top right: Beef stock Bottom: Béchamel sauce

Béchamel sauce

MAKES ABOUT 300 ml (½ pint)

300 ml (½ pint) milk
1 small onion, roughly chopped
1 carrot, sliced
1 small celery stalk, sliced
1 bay leaf
3 whole black peppercorns
25 g (1 oz) butter
25 g (1 oz) cornflour
salt and pepper

Place the milk, onion, carrot, celery, bay leaf and peppercorns in a saucepan. Bring to the boil, then remove from the heat, cover and leave to infuse for 20 minutes. Strain.

Melt the butter in a small saucepan. Stir in the cornflour and cook gently for 2 minutes, stirring constantly. Remove from the heat and gradually add the strained milk, stirring or whisking until the sauce is smooth. Return to the heat, bring to the boil, stirring, then reduce the heat and simmer for 3 minutes until the sauce is thickened. Season to taste with salt and pepper.

To freeze: Cool quickly and pour into rigid containers, in small quantities if desired. Cover, seal, label and freeze for up to 6 months.
To serve: Turn the frozen sauce into a saucepan, add 2 tbls milk and reheat gently for about 30 minutes, stirring and turning the block occasionally. A good basic white sauce, Béchamel is also used as the base for other sauces.
Variations: Cheese – add 50 g (2 oz) grated Cheddar cheese and 1 tsp prepared mustard.
Mushroom – add 100 g (4 oz) thinly sliced mushrooms, lightly fried in 50 g (2 oz) butter.
Prawn – add 50 g (2 oz) cooked peeled prawns, 1 tbls tomato purée and 1 tsp lemon juice.
Parsley – add 3 tablespoons of finely chopped fresh green parsley and a dash of lemon juice.

Tomato sauce

MAKES 1.2 litres (2 pints)

4 tbls vegetable oil
2 onions, chopped
2 garlic cloves, crushed
1.5 kg (3 lb) ripe tomatoes, skinned and chopped or 3 × 397 g (14 oz) cans tomatoes, drained
2 tsp sugar
2 tbls tomato purée
2 tsp dried thyme
2 bay leaves
300 ml (½ pint) Beef stock (see page 60)
salt and pepper

Heat the oil in a heavy-based saucepan, add the onions and garlic and fry over low heat for 2-3 minutes, or until transparent. Add the tomatoes and all the remaining ingredients. Season to taste with salt and pepper.

Bring to the boil, stir well, then cover, reduce the heat and simmer gently for 30 minutes, stirring occasionally.

Remove the bay leaves and purée the sauce in a blender or food processor. Return to the saucepan and simmer gently, uncovered, for about 20 minutes or until reduced.

To freeze: Cool quickly and pour into rigid containers, in small quantities if desired. Cover, seal, label and freeze for up to 1 year.
To serve: Turn the frozen sauce into a saucepan, add 2 tbls water and reheat gently for 30 minutes, stirring and turning the block occasionally.

Mint sauce

MAKES ABOUT 175 ml (6 fl oz)

When mint is threatening to overrun your garden, pick and freeze some in handy cubes. Chop the mint finely, mix with boiling water (1 tbls mint to 1 tbls water), cool and freeze in an ice-cube tray. When solid, store the cubes in a polythene bag. Each cube, thawed, will yield about 1 tbls.

8 mint cubes, thawed
1 tbls caster sugar
4 tbls white wine vinegar

Thaw the mint cubes in a small sauceboat, stir in the sugar and vinegar and allow to stand for about 1 hour before serving.

• Left to right: Mint sauce; Tomato sauce; Apple sauce; Chocolate sauce

Apple sauce

MAKES ABOUT 250 ml (8 fl oz)

450 g (1 lb) cooking apples, peeled, cored and sliced
50 ml (2 fl oz) water
25 g (1 oz) butter
salt and pepper

Place the apples, water and butter in a non-stick saucepan. Bring to the boil, reduce the heat, cover and simmer, stirring occasionally, for about 15 minutes or until the apples are soft and fluffy. Beat with a wooden spoon to make a smooth purée. Season with salt and pepper.

To freeze: Cool quickly and pack into small containers. Seal, label and freeze for up to 6 months.
To serve: Thaw, covered, for 4 hours at room temperature and serve cold. Or melt 15 g (½ oz) butter in a saucepan, add the frozen sauce and reheat gently for about 15 minutes, stirring and turning the block occasionally. Serve with pork, duck or goose.
Variations: If you like your apple sauce sweet, add 1 tbs caster sugar with the apples when cooking. For a hint of spice, add 4-5 cloves with the apples but remove before serving.

Chocolate sauce

MAKES ABOUT 300 ml (½ pint)

75 g (3 oz) caster sugar
1 tsp vanilla essence
2 tsp cornflour
300 ml (½ pint) milk
50 g (2 oz) plain chocolate, broken into pieces
25 g (1 oz) butter

Place the sugar and vanilla essence in a saucepan.

In a cup, blend the cornflour with a little of the milk to make a smooth paste. Stir the cornflour mixture into the saucepan with the remaining milk. Stir over a gentle heat until the sugar has dissolved, then increase the heat and boil briskly, without stirring, for 2 minutes. Remove from the heat, add the chocolate and butter and stir until thoroughly blended and glossy.

To freeze: Cool quickly, pour into rigid containers, seal, label and freeze for up to 3 months.
To serve: Turn the frozen sauce into a heavy-based saucepan, add 1 tbls milk and reheat gently for about 15 minutes, stirring and turning the block.
Variations: The vanilla essence may be replaced by rum or brandy.

INDEX

Note: this index includes variations suggested in recipes as well as the main recipes